BBQ BISTRO

SIMPLE, SOPHISTICATED FRENCH RECIPES FOR YOUR GRILL

Karen Adler & Judith Fertig

authors of
The Gardener & the Grill

RUNNING PRESS
PHILADELPHIA · LONDON

© 2015 by Karen Adler and Judith Fertig
Photography © 2015 by Steve Legato

Published by Running Press,
A Member of the Perseus Books Group

Printed in China

Books published by Running Press are available at special discounts for bulk purchases
in the United States by corporations, institutions, and other organizations.
For more information, please contact the Special Markets Department at the Perseus Books Group,
2300 Chestnut Street, Suite 200, Philadelphia, PA 19103, or call (800) 810-4145, ext. 5000,
or e-mail special.markets@perseusbooks.com.

ISBN 978-0-7624-5454-9
Library of Congress Control Number: 2014956652

E-book ISBN 978-0-7624-5603-1

9 8 7 6 5 4 3 2 1
Digit on the right indicates the number of this printing

Designed by Frances J. Soo Ping Chow
Edited by Sophia Muthuraj
Food Stylist: Mariana Velasquez
Prop Stylist: Mariellen Melker
Typography: Chronicle Text, Gin, Phaeton, Sentinel,
Stereopticon, and Trade Gothic

Running Press Book Publishers
2300 Chestnut Street
Philadelphia, PA 19103-4371

Visit us on the web!
www.offthemenublog.com

TO ALL OUR FRIENDS, FAMILY, AND COLLEAGUES
NEAR AND DEAR WHO INSPIRE US,
BREAK BREAD WITH US, AND GATHER ROUND THE GRILL.

LA VIE EST DÉLICIEUSE!

TABLE OF CONTENTS

We have both enjoyed many a bistro meal on our travels, especially when we have lived and cooked in France. We love the vibrant colors, the casual atmosphere, and the vintage feel at the French equivalent of a mom-and-pop restaurant, where the cooks know what they're doing, the *plat du jour* is the blue plate special, and your glass is filled with wine. We love the zinc-topped bars, black-and-white tile flooring, and robust food served on plain white china, with a Gallic flair to it all.

We always go home, however, and as women who barbecue outdoors and cook indoors, we have thought about how we could translate the bistro dishes that we have enjoyed to food on the grill.

Now, it seems, reinventing bistro food is on trend.

Recently, chefs from Montreal to New York, Seattle to Paris have been reinventing bistro food by tweaking the classics and cooking over higher heat on planks, a rotisserie, or over a wood fire.

Voilà! That's *BBQ Bistro.*

Traditional bistro food, French fast food, usually features a thin cut of meat or fish, such as a chicken paillard or a salmon fillet. For us, *BBQ Bistro* is a hot and fast grill plus a sophisticated French sauce like Mustard-Cornichon Beurre Blanc (page 38) to finish. And for more vegetables-as-center-of-the-plate, Grilled Cauliflower Paillards with Orange-Olive Pistou (page 113), Vegetable Paillards with French Feta Spread (page 117), or Provençal-Style Stuffed Smoked Vegetables (page 116) give traditional French bistro foods a lighter, updated barbecue twist.

The "small plates" concept also works with bistro, as Jody Williams's *gastrothèque* Buvette proves successfully in New York City *and* Paris. In either place, you can enjoy a *Croque forestiere* (a grilled mushroom sandwich) with a glass of wine, any time of day. You can do the same with a Croque Monsieur on the Grill Griddle (page 93) and a glass of wine and save the airfare.

Tartines (grilled bread with toppings) and socca—that delicious chickpea flatbread served in the south of France—all taste better on the grill. According to Francophile David Lebovitz, "Although you can make it at home, making socca in a home oven is like baking off a batch of s'mores in there: It's close, but not exactly the real thing. You really do need a wood-fire to get that blistered crust." Your grill and a cast-iron skillet will give you a much more authentic result than the stovetop or oven.

Parisian bistro chefs are rediscovering spit-roasted chicken, grilled to an herb-buttered deliciousness that you can only get over an open flame. Many of those same rotisserie bistros also offer planked poultry, game, and fish. Try our Spit-Roasted Chicken with Charred Tomatoes on the Vine (page 129), Planked Chicken Breasts with Artichoke Slather (page 131), or Planked Scallops with Pistachio Butter (page 45) for a taste of France as close as your own backyard.

On the grill, you can get a char on a steak, a smoky flavor on cheese, or a roasted-ness you thought could only be done at a restaurant.

To increase your grilling savoir faire, *BBQ Bistro* offers an array of barbecue techniques:

- High heat grilling
- Grilling on a plancha, plank, or cast iron
- Grilling vegetables so they can claim the center of the plate
- Rotisserie grilling
- Grill-roasting
- Wood or herb grilling
- Grilling with a kiss of smoke

All of this reaches back to the hearth-style cooking of long ago and blazes ahead to the lighter, fresher way we want to eat now, all with a French twist.

According to Judy Rogers, the late doyenne of the famed Zuni Café in San Francisco, the multi-Michelin-starred Claude Troisgros "loved steak frites at the local café better than going to a three-star restaurant. It is pretty clear that the food you eat every day is the most important food." So, let's make everyday, home-style food as delicious as possible. Let's pick it fresh from the garden, flavor it with herbs and spice and wine. Let's give it the depth that only wood smoke can give it. Let's choose the freshest fish and seafood and beautiful aged steaks to sear on the grill and pair with lovely French sauces. Let's slow smoke larger cuts of meat until they are melt-in-your-mouth tender like the Smoky Lamb Daube (page 148) and the Provençal Beef Daube (page 170).

Let's take it outside.

Let's make it *BBQ Bistro*.

GRILLING IS A MATTER OF DEGREES

You can do a lot more with your grill than simply sear: You can melt, toast, scorch, blacken, add a kiss of smoke, spit-roast, plank, and grill in a flash. But first you need a grill.

GAS OR CHARCOAL GRILL?

People always ask us if we grill with charcoal or gas, to which we answer yes—we use both. The majority of American households have at least one outdoor grill, which, more often than not, is gas rather than charcoal. As far as we're concerned, to get great flavor and char, charcoal is the way to go—in particular, hardwood lump charcoal, which burns really hot for a terrific sear. But there are pluses to gas grilling as well, not the least of which is you just flip a switch and it's on. You can add wood smoke to a gas grill, too, as we'll show you later on. Just make sure you buy a unit with as high a number of BTUs (British Thermal Units, which measure the maximum heat output of a burner) as your budget permits for hot surface searing. You'll need at least 40,000 BTUs from the grill burners (not including any side burners' BTUs) to get good grill marks on your foods.

CLEANING AND MAINTENANCE

A STIFF WIRE BRUSH with a scraper makes cleaning the grill easy. Tackle this while the grill is still warm.

ONE NATURAL-BRISTLE BASTING BRUSH can be used to apply oil to the grill and a second to baste food during grilling or smoking.

GRATE CHEF GRILL WIPES are small pads saturated with high-temperature cooking oil. You can use them for oiling the grill grates prior to cooking, then turn them over to clean the grill when you're finished cooking. The high-temperature oil doesn't smoke, and it doesn't drip from the pads, which prevents flare-ups.

UTENSILS FOR *BBQ BISTRO*

Several basic tools make grilling easier. Kitchen shops, hardware stores, restaurant supply stores, and barbecue and grill retailers are good sources of the items listed below. Professional utensils are superior in quality and durability and worth the extra money. Long handles are preferable on everything, to keep you a safe distance from the fire.

PERFORATED GRILL RACKS are placed on top of the grill grates to accommodate small or delicate food items (such as chicken wings, fish fillets, shellfish, and vegetables) that might fall through the grates. Always oil the grill rack before using so that the food won't stick.

CAST-IRON SKILLETS, OVEN-PROOF SKILLETS, AND GRILL GRIDDLES are great for grilling flatbreads, steaks, chops, and fish fillets on the grill.

GRILL WOKS AND BASKETS WITH PERFORATED HOLES let in smoky flavor while sitting directly on top of the grill. Stir-grill fish, chicken, or shellfish and vegetables by tossing them with long-handled wooden paddles.

HEAT-RESISTANT OVEN OR GRILL MITTS offer the best hand protection, especially when you need to touch any hot metal, such as skewers, during the grilling process.

LONG-HANDLED, SPRING-LOADED TONGS are easier to use than the scissors type. They are great for turning shellfish, sliced vegetables, and skewers. Buy two sets of tongs—one for raw meats and the other for cooked meats.

LONG-HANDLED OFFSET SPATULAS with extra-long spatula surfaces are great for turning large pieces of food, fish fillets, long planks of eggplant, zucchini, or yellow squash. Oil the food well to avoid sticking.

Keep a **SPRAY BOTTLE** or pan filled with water handy to douse big flare-ups. (Little flare-ups add that bit of desirable char and you want to be careful not to put out the fire.)

SKEWERS—wooden or metal—allow smaller items to be threaded loosely together and then placed on the grill to cook. Wooden or bamboo skewers should be soaked for at least 30 minutes before using so that the ends won't char during grilling. Flat wooden or metal skewers are preferred, so that cubed food doesn't spin while turning. Or use double skewers to keep cubed food from spinning.

DISPOSABLE ALUMINUM PANS are perfect for grilling a medley of vegetables or catching the drippings under a spit-roasted chicken.

We like to have an **INSTANT-READ THERMOMETER** handy by the grill to test the doneness of beef, chicken, lamb, pork, turkey, and breads.

A **CHARCOAL CHIMNEY** or electric fire starter is key for starting a charcoal fire.

A good-quality **CHEF'S KNIFE** is essential for preparing vegetables, fruits, herbs, and other foods destined for the grill.

SIMPLE GRILLING

_❧

LIGHTING THE FIRE

Charcoal Grills

A charcoal fire can be started in any of several safe, ecologically sound ways. We prefer using real hardwood lump charcoal instead of compressed charcoal briquettes. It is readily available at most barbecue and grill shops, hardware stores with large grill departments, and some grocery stores. It gives a better flavor and is an all-natural product without chemical additives. It also burns hotter, which is desirable for high-heat grilling.

You can start your hardwood lump charcoal in a metal charcoal chimney or with an electric fire starter, both available at hardware, barbecue, and home improvement stores and most gourmet shops.

LIGHTING THE FIRE WITH A CHARCOAL CHIMNEY. It is easy to start a charcoal grill with just a match, newspaper, and charcoal. The only special equipment you need is an upright cylindrical metal canister, which looks like a large metal coffee can with a handle. Fill it with fifteen to twenty pieces of hardwood lump charcoal, and then place it on a nonflammable surface, such as concrete, gravel, or the grill rack. Slightly tip the chimney over and stuff one or two crumpled sheets of newspaper in the convex-shaped bottom. Light the paper with a match. After 5 minutes, check to make sure that the charcoal has caught fire, or you may need to light another piece of newspaper under the chimney again.

It takes about 15 to 20 minutes for the coals to flame. When the flames subside and the coals are glowing red and just beginning to ash over, it's time to carefully pour the coals onto the fire grates. You can add more charcoal to the fire if you need to, but wait until the new charcoal has begun to ash over before cooking. Start a charcoal grill about 20 to 30 minutes before you're ready to grill.

LIGHTING THE FIRE WITH ELECTRICITY. An electric fire starter is another easy way to start a fire in a charcoal grill. You'll need an outdoor electrical outlet or extension cord. Place the coil on the fire rack of the grill and stack charcoal on top of it. Plug it in and the fire will start in about 10 to 15 minutes. Remove the coil and let the starter cool on a nonflammable surface, out of the reach of children and pets.

Preparing a Direct Fire

In this book, when we tell you to "prepare a medium-hot fire in your grill," this means direct heat, with the flames under the food you're cooking.

To create "direct fire" make sure the bottom vents of the grill are open, as fire needs oxygen. Next, start a fire in a charcoal chimney using hardwood lump charcoal and newspaper or use an electric fire starter. Place more hardwood charcoal in the bottom of the grill. When the coals are hot in the charcoal chimney, dump them on top of the charcoal in the bottom of the grill and wait for all the coals to catch fire and ash over. Your fire should extend out about 2 inches (5 cm) beyond the space you will need for the food you plan to grill. When they've just begun to ash over and turn a whitish gray, replace the grill grate. Place the food on the grill grate, directly over the coals.

DONENESS CHART FOR GRILLING

Personal preferences run the gamut from very rare to very well done.
Use this chart as a guideline for your outdoor grilling.

Sandwiches . . . . Good grill marks or warmed through to your liking

Tartines . . . . Good grill marks

Vegetables . . . . Good grill marks and done to your liking

Fruits . . . . Good grill marks and done to your liking

Beef . . . . 125°F/45°C for rare, 140°F/60°C for medium, 160°F/75°C for well done

Chicken breast . . . . 160°F/75°C

Turkey breast . . . . 165°F/77°C

Fish fillet . . . . Begins to flake when tested with a fork in thickest part

Shellfish . . . . Opaque and somewhat firm to the touch

Lamb . . . . 125°F/45°C for rare, 140°F/60°C for medium

Pork . . . . 140°F/60°C for medium, 160°F/75°C for well done

Preparing an Indirect Fire

When we tell you to "prepare a medium-hot indirect fire in your grill," this means no heat on one side of the grill and heat on the other side.

Prepare a direct fire first, as instructed on page 11. Once your hot coals are in the bottom of the grill, there are two ways you can create an indirect fire. First, using a long-handled grill spatula, push the coals over to one side of the grill to provide direct heat there. The other side of the grill will now have indirect heat. Second, bank the coals on both sides of the grill. The center of the grill will then be the indirect cooking area. Place the hardwood chunks, chips, or pellets (for wood smoke flavoring) on top of the coals. Replace the grill grate.

With an indirect fire, you can grill directly over the hot coals while you smoke over the indirect side. When cooking indirectly, close the grill lid and use the vents on the top and bottom of the grill to adjust the fire temperature. Open vents allow more oxygen in and make the fire hotter, partially closed vents lower the heat, and closed vents extinguish the fire.

Gas Grills

LIGHTING THE GAS GRILL. Follow the manufacturer's directions for starting your gas grill. The manufacturer's directions will tell you how long your grill takes to reach the temperature you want. Newer grills have inset thermometers that register the temperature inside the grill.

Preparing a Direct Fire

Turn the burners on. Place the food on the grill grate directly over the hot burner, and that is direct heat. To cook this way, ideally leave the grill lid up. When it is raining or snowing, however, closing the lid is preferable. This will essentially turn the hot grill into a hot oven, meaning you'll actually be grill-roasting.

Preparing an Indirect Fire

Your grill must have at least two burners for indirect grilling, preferably side by side burners. Fire up the burner on one half of the grill only. The side of the grill with the burner off is for indirect cooking or for quickly moving food off the heat. To cook this way as with Lavender-Smoked Rack of Lamb (page 145), close the grill lid. If you have three or more burners, you may also set up your grill with the two outer burners on and the center of your grill used for indirect cooking. Adjust the burners to regulate the level of heat.

GRILL WITH THE LID OPEN OR SHUT?

Traditionally, grilling was done over an open fire or flame. For some recipes in this book, you'll grill with the lid open, as in Bistro Chicken Paillards (page 128), Grilled Baby Artichokes with Parmesan and Lemon Drizzle (page 49), or Char-Grilled Romaine, Bacon, Tomato, and Roquefort (page 74). But sometimes, closing the lid allows you to build up more heat, get more wood smoke flavor in the food, or grill-roast.

GRILLING TEMPERATURE

Most food is grilled directly over a medium-hot to hot fire, depending on the distance your grill rack sits from the fire and the heat of the fire itself.

In a charcoal grill, the fire is ready when the flames have subsided and the coals are glowing red and just beginning to ash over. This is a hot fire. You can recognize a medium-hot fire when the coals are no longer red but instead are ashen.

For a gas grill, read the manufacturer's directions for the time it takes the grill to reach the desired temperature. Or use a grill thermometer to judge the grill's temperature.

ADJUSTING YOUR GRILL'S TEMPERATURE

On a charcoal grill, always begin the fire with the bottom or side vents open. Lower the temperature by partially closing the vents, and raise the temperature by opening the vents or by adding more charcoal to ratchet up the fire. More air means the fire will burn faster and hotter; less air makes for a slower and lower temperature fire.

On a gas grill, adjust the heat by turning the heat control knobs to the desired level. Most heat control knobs are marked "high," "medium," and "low," although some are marked only "high" and "low." On some models, you can control the temperature by turning the temperature dial.

HOW TO GRILL

Once your grill is at the proper temperature, follow our recipe directions for grilling. Good grill marks are desirable and accomplished by searing and charring before turning the foods with grill tongs or a grill spatula. Avoid turning the food unless the recipe says to do so. The food needs to sit undisturbed for a time to get those lovely grill marks.

FRENCH WOODS FOR
WOOD-GRILLING AND SMOKING

The wood you use in barbecue is all about local availability, which is why maple is more popular in New England, hickory is big in the Carolinas, pecan and mesquite are beloved in Texas, and oak and apple woods have a following in Kansas City. In France, it's the same way. We once had a fabulous meal at L'Orée d'Opio near Nice in the south of France, where Chef Erick Bernard prepared each dish in a wood-fired oven, using local chestnut wood or *châtaigne*. When obtaining chestnut wood, you may find untreated chestnut wood at a lumber yard (call first), but your best bet is knowing someone who has a chestnut tree and getting dead branches from them. The French term for cooking with a wood fire is *cuisine au feu de bois*, and those woods could include the following:

- Almond gives a nutty, sweet flavor similar to pecan wood that is good with most foods.
- Apple and other fruitwoods like peach and pear give a sweet, aromatic flavor good with chicken and pork.
- Cherry provides a deeper, sweeter flavor good with beef tenderloin, pork, chicken, and game.
- Chestnut emits a rich, smoky flavor and is good with game, beef, pork, and lamb.
- Grapevines give a lighter, aromatic flavor good with fish, shellfish, and chicken.
- Maple has a mild flavor and marries well with poultry and pork.
- Oak and oak wine barrel staves give a medium smoky flavor that pairs well with lamb, game, poultry, and pork.
- Orange wafts a lighter, sweeter aromatic flavor than other fruitwoods like apple or cherry.
- Pecan wood is nutty and spicy, making it a perfect choice for poultry, pork, fish, and shellfish.
- Rosemary and lavender stalks give a woodsy aroma and are good with breads, fish, shellfish, lamb, pork, beef, and game.

WHEN IS YOUR FOOD DONE ON THE GRILL?

Vegetables, tartines, sandwiches, and fruits are done when they have good grill marks or they're tender enough for your liking. Easy.

We recommend that if you're just starting to grill, you use an instant-read meat thermometer to test the doneness of grilled chicken, pork, beef, veal, lamb, and breads. Insert the thermometer in the thickest part of the meat or bread and read the temperature. After a while, you'll be able to tell the doneness of grilled foods by look, smell, and touch. When you touch a beef tenderloin with tongs and it's soft and wiggly, it's too rare. When the tenderloin begins to offer some resistance, it's rare to medium-rare. When it just begins to firm up, it's medium. When it feels solid, it's well done. For exact temperatures and a great guide to knowing when meat is cooked, please see the handy chart on page 11.

WOOD GRILLING AND KISS OF SMOKE

To get more wood smoke flavor from your grill, you simply add hardwood to the fire, as you will in Smoked Goat Cheese Salad with Sweet Cherries (page 77), Wood-Grilled Oysters with Smoky Bacon (page 43), or Provençal Beef Daube (page 170).

A QUICK KISS OF SMOKE. On a charcoal grill, you could add small, seasoned branches of hardwood like oak, maple, or pecan; fruitwoods like apple, pear, or peach; or even dried grapevines or woody herb stalks like rosemary or lavender. You simply add a branch or two, several wood chunks, or a handful of wood chips to the fire after the coals have ashed over.

You want to wait to put your food on until you see the first wisp of smoke (so you know the wood is smoldering and you'll get the wood smoke flavor you want). Then, simply place your food on the grill grate, close the lid, and let the food smoke and grill at the same time.

For a gas grill, you want to avoid any debris getting into the gas jets, so you'll want to contain the wood in a homemade aluminum foil packet or in a metal smoker box you can buy at barbecue shops, gourmet stores with barbecue accessories, or hardware stores. We find that dry wood chips smolder more quickly, so simply place a large handful fine of wood chips or wood pellets (available at barbecue shops, gourmet stores with barbecue accessories, or hardware stores) in an aluminum foil packet or metal smoker box. Poke holes in the packet (the smoker box already has perforations).

Place the packet or smoker box close to a fired gas jet, using grill tongs. When you see the first wisp of smoke, simply place your food on the grill grate, close the lid, and let the food smoke and grill at the same time.

The wood chips or pellets will smolder rather than burn, adding smoky flavor for about 1 hour.

A LINGERING KISS OF SMOKE. For foods that need a longer kiss of smoke, we recommend using wood chunks for a charcoal grill. These are 3 to 5-inch (7.5 to 12-cm) pieces of hardwood packaged in bags and available at barbecue and hardware stores. These larger pieces smolder more slowly to flavor foods that need 1 to 3 hours to get a smoky flavor.

For a charcoal grill, you simply place the wood chunks on the ashed-over coals.

For a gas grill, you place the wood chips in a foil packet, poke holes in the top to let the smoke out, and place the packet near a burner so the wood will smolder. Replenish the wood chips as needed for additional smoke.

THE ART OF EN BROCHETTE

For grilling foods on a skewer in the French style, you can use wood or bamboo skewers, campfire sticks (that you pick up in your yard), fresh rosemary or lavender herb branches, or metal skewers. Wooden (bamboo) skewers, which come in packages at the grocery store, need to be soaked in water for at least 30 minutes before threading them with food and grilling. After grilling, you just throw the charred skewers away.

SIMPLE STIR-GRILLING

Stir-grilling foods over a hot fire is a great way to show off your vegetable harvest—and no mess in the kitchen! We include this technique because it increases your grilling savoir faire. You can, if you wish, serve stir-grilled vegetables atop pasta or couscous, but they're also terrific on their own.

To stir-grill, you need a grill wok, a hexagonal metal wok with perforations, along with wooden spoons, paddles, or long-handled spatulas. The perforations in the wok allow for more of the grill flavors to penetrate the food. Grill woks are usually 12 to 15 inches/30 to 37.5 cm in size. We prefer a bigger wok because more space means potentially more grill flavor and more room for a larger quantity of food. We like to use long-handled wooden paddles or spoons to toss the food in a grill wok. We call this technique "stir-grilling," a similar but healthier alternative to stir-frying.

PLANKING OR GRILLING A LA PLANCHA

Plank cooking is easy, too. You can buy untreated hardwood planks at a lumberyard or barbecue shop. The most common planks come in several sizes, the most common being 15 x 6½ x 8 inches (37 x 16 x 20 cm). Use whatever size best fits on your grill. We also use those 2- to 3-inch-thick (5 to 7.5 cm) reinforced cedar planks (made for oven use but also great on the grill) available at kitchen or barbecue and grill shops. Food cooks in about the same time on thinner or thicker planks, but thicker planks last longer. Planks can be reused until they're either too charred or too brittle to hold food.

Although planking on cedar is the universal favorite as it gives the best aromatic flavor, any regional hardwood—such as alder, hickory, maple, oak, or pecan—will produce great-tasting planked food, too. A simple test is to sniff the plank. If you can't smell any aromatic wood, it's not going to impart flavor to your food. Go for the plank with the best aroma.

To use the plank, submerge it in water for at least an hour. A deep sink or a large rectangular plastic container that you can fill with water both work. Use a couple of large cans to weigh down the plank so that it stays under the surface. A water-soaked plank produces maximum smoke flavor and is more resistant to charring on the grill.

Prepare an indirect (high or medium-high on one side, no heat on the other) fire in your grill. You can do this with a gas grill with dual burners or in a charcoal grill by massing the hot coals on the "hot" side. For wider charcoal grills or gas grills with three burners, you can make the indirect part in the middle, with coals or lit burners on each side.

The part of the food that touches the wood plank takes on more flavor, so don't crowd the food onto the plank. Use two planks, if necessary. Then close the grill lid and cook according to the time specified in the recipe. Stay close by, though, in case of flare-ups. Keep a spray bottle filled with water handy, just in case.

For a rustic bistro effect, serve the food right on the plank, like a platter. After you've cooked and served on the plank, clean it up with a little hot, soapy water and a good rinse. Eighty-grit sandpaper may be used to help clean the plank, too. Let it air dry and store in a cupboard uncovered.

HARDWOOD FLAVORS FOR PLANKING

Thinner grilling planks come in variety of hardwoods at your local hardware store, barbecue and grilling shop, or big box store. Thicker oven planks are generally cedar and are available at barbecue and grilling stores or kitchenware shops.

- Alder gives a light, aromatic flavor and is great paired with fish.
- Cedar is probably the most aromatic of the woods, lending a deep but gentle woodsy flavor to planked foods of all kinds.
- Hickory lends a stronger, hearty wood flavor to beef, pork, or poultry.
- Maple smolders to a sweeter, milder flavor that pairs well with poultry, vegetables, or fish.
- Oak gives a medium, woodsy aroma without being bitter. It also pairs well with any food.

CAST-IRON GRILLING

Cast-iron griddles or skillets, heated to a high temperature on the grill, can sear a great steak or a fish fillet, turn out a fabulous Croque Monsieur on the Grill Griddle (page 93), and griddle-bake a delicious Socca on the Grill (page 55).

First, heat the griddle or skillet with the grill lid closed for about 20 minutes or until it is very hot.

Brush the filet mignon on both sides with oil and grill on the griddle or in the skillet, uncovered, for 2 to 3 minutes per side, turning once for a charry, black and bleu steak.

For fish, brush both sides of the fish fillet with oil, place on the griddle or in the skillet, close the grill lid, and grill for 3 to 4 minutes, turning once, or until the fish begins to flake when tested with a fork in the thickest part.

ROTISSERIE GRILLING

To spit-roast or rotisserie, first set up your rotisserie on the grill. A gas grill with an electric, self-turning rotisserie attachment is the simplest way to go. Every gas grill has a different way to set up a rotisserie, so we're just giving you an overview here. Please refer to your manufacturer's directions for the best way to set up the rotisserie on your grill. The drip pan should contain 2 to 3 inches (5 to 7.5 cm) of liquid—marinades, vinegar, juice, beer, wine, or just plain water—whatever you would like for aroma. The liquid will steam up into the food, adding moisture and a wonderful aroma as the food turns and cooks. Replenish with additional liquid as necessary.

Run through your setup first. Do not skewer the food and place it on a lit grill until you are certain that everything is set properly. With the grill off or unlit, measure the food over the drip pan. The pan will prevent flare-ups, so make sure the meat, chicken, or fish is not larger than the drip pan you are planning to use. If it is, use either a larger pan or an additional drip pan. For easy cleanup, we prefer to use a disposable aluminum pan.

Trim the meat, poultry, or fish and then season it. If you're using the rotisserie basket (great for fish or other delicate foods), spray it with nonstick cooking spray, place the food inside the basket, and close firmly. Slide one of the pronged attachments or spit forks onto the rotisserie rod. Position the attachment and clamp to tighten. Slide the rod through the center of the meat, fish, or fowl. Slide the second prong attachment so that the tines are touching the food. Holding a prong attachment in each hand, press both attachments into the food so that the food is held firmly in place. Secure and tighten the clamps for the pronged attachments. Use pliers to tighten the thumbscrews on the spit forks to prevent loosening during the rotisserie process.

Balancing the Food on the Spit

It's very important to balance the meat on the spit so it can turn easily. If the meat is not balanced, it could shorten the life of your rotisserie. To balance the rod, hold it so each end lies across the palms of your hands; the heavy side of the food will rotate down. Position the food on the rod so that there is no heavy side.

Tie any loose bits to the body of the meat with kitchen string. Insert a meat thermometer in the thickest part of the meat, away from the bone. Make sure that the thermometer is positioned so that you can read it and also so that it will turn freely as the meat turns.

Place the spit on the rotisserie. Start the rotisserie, letting it rotate enough times until you're sure the meat turns easily. Place the drip pan under the food. Add liquid to the drip pan until it is 2 to 3 inches (5 to 7.5 cm) full. This helps keep the food moist and prevents the drippings from burning.

Check to make sure the grill's lid will close while the rotisserie is on. If necessary, you can prop the grill lid open a bit with bricks or metal cans.

Prepare a medium-hot fire in your grill. Check with a grill thermometer to make sure you have achieved a temperature of close to 350°F (180°C). Cover and cook, checking the meat, the fire, and the drip pan at least every hour. You may need to add liquid to the drip pan during cooking. Sometimes the thumbscrews can loosen, or the meat may shrink and the forks may need to be adjusted, so keep a clean pair of pliers handy just in case you need to make some adjustments. When the food is done, lift the rotisserie and food off the grill. Place the whole thing on a baking sheet, then remove the rod and proceed to retrieve your food.

GARDE-MANGER
PANTRY

The French term for pantry—*garde-manger*—translates into "keeper of the food" or the place where food is kept. In French restaurants, the chef who takes on *garde-manger* duty has a tough job with many moving parts, but in a griller's household, this simply means making seasonings and sauces ahead of time.

You don't want to be out at the grill, searing the perfect steak, and think, "*Saint-merde,* I forgot to make the Béarnaise!"

From herb rubs, salts, and grilling paste to traditional *pistou* (the French version of pesto), this chapter showcases lots of ways to get robust flavor before grilling, smoking, or planking. Vinaigrettes do double duty as marinades and finishing sauces for vegetables. And then aioli, Lime-Cilantro Remoulade (page 32), and cream sauces like Lemon-Tarragon Cream Sauce (page 34) pair well with grilled foods of all kinds and can be made well ahead of time.

The emulsion sauces—Béarnaise Sauce (page 36), Mustard-Cornichon Beurre Blanc (page 38), Three-Peppercorn Beurre Blanc (page 39)—are based in the classic French tradition but updated for today. Once made, keep them warm with the pan set over hot water. Don't try to keep them going for more than 30 minutes.

You can also grill and smoke vegetables ahead of time and keep them ready to pop into sauces, sandwiches, soups, or salads. See The Bistro Grill Pantry (page 37) and The *BBQ Bistro* Smoke Pantry (page 30) for how to do that.

PROVENÇAL HERB RUB

THE DRY, CHALKY HILLSIDES IN THE SOUTH OF FRANCE PRODUCE HERBS WITH A high volatile oil content, which translates to more aroma and flavor. Try this blend on fish, meat, and vegetables. We both keep an ever-changing dried herb jar in our kitchens, which receives the addition of a new herb at whim. Customize a jar by combining your favorite dried herbs. Use 1 to 2 teaspoons of this rub per fish fillet or steak. You can find dried lavender buds online at Penzeys or from other herb and spice shops.

MAKES ¾ CUP (175 ML)

3 tablespoons dried thyme

3 tablespoons dried rosemary

3 dried bay leaves

2 tablespoons dried basil

2 tablespoons dried marjoram

1½ teaspoons fennel seeds

1 teaspoon dried summer savory

1 teaspoon dried lavender buds
(culinary use only)

Combine the ingredients, leaving the bay leaves whole. Prepare at least 1 hour ahead of time so the bay leaves have time to infuse the mixture with their flavor. Store in a dark cupboard in a glass jar with a tight-fitting lid; it will keep its punch for up to 6 months. Remove the bay leaves before using the blend, then return the bay leaves to the mixture after use.

THREE-PEPPERCORN RUB

PEPPERCORNS IN THREE DIFFERENT COLORS AND FLAVORS MEAN THREE TIMES THE flavor in this rub, which is delicious on the classic *steak au poivre* (page 164). You'll need a mortar and pestle (or a clean dish towel and a heavy meat mallet) to crack but not completely grind the toasted peppercorns. For an even greater hit of peppercorn, serve grilled beef, salmon, or tuna steaks with this rub, accompanied by Three-Peppercorn Beurre Blanc (page 39).

MAKES ABOUT 1/3 CUP (75 ML)

2 tablespoons Szechuan or white peppercorns

2 tablespoons black peppercorns

1 tablespoon dried green peppercorns

1 tablespoon coarse kosher or sea salt

Place all the ingredients in a small cast-iron skillet over medium-high heat and toast, stirring frequently, until the spices become aromatic, about 2 minutes.

Scrape the mixture into a mortar and grind it with a pestle until crushed and still somewhat coarse. Use right away.

FRENCH HERB GARDEN SALTS

A heady, aromatic herb salt adds flavor to foods before or after grilling. The flavor of these salts gets better after a day or two, so plan ahead. Untreated or organic lavender buds are available at health food stores, online, or from your favorite gardener.

Rosemary Salt is delicious on vegetables or beef; Lavender Salt on chicken or lamb; and Fennel Salt on fish and shellfish.

Makes about ¼ cup (50 ml)

2 tablespoons dried rosemary, dried lavender buds (culinary use only), or fennel seeds

2 tablespoons fleur de sel or coarse sea salt

Combine the ingredients in a small glass jar with a tight-fitting lid. Cover and shake to blend. The salt will keep in the cupboard for several months.

VARIATIONS:

To make Lavender Salt: Substitute culinary dried lavender buds for the rosemary.

To make Fennel Salt: Substitute fennel seeds for the rosemary.

WALNUT OIL VINAIGRETTE

THIS IS DELICIOUS DRIZZLED OVER GRILLED VEGETABLES, CHICKEN, LAMB, OR PORK and is especially wonderful with salads that have toasted walnuts and grilled fruit as ingredients. Walnut oil is available at gourmet shops, olive oil stores, and specialty markets. Once opened, keep the walnut oil in the refrigerator.

MAKES 1 CUP (250 ML)

1/3 cup (75 ml) walnut oil

1/3 cup (75 ml) extra-virgin olive oil

1/3 cup (75 ml) balsamic vinegar

1 tablespoon minced onion

2 teaspoons Dijon mustard

1 teaspoon granulated sugar

1/2 teaspoon kosher salt

In a glass jar with a tight-fitting lid, combine the walnut oil, olive oil, vinegar, onion, mustard, sugar, and salt; cover and shake to blend. Use right away or store in refrigerator for up to 2 weeks.

LEMON–TARRAGON VINAIGRETTE

AS A MARINADE OR A FINISHING SAUCE, THIS IS DYNAMITE WITH CHICKEN, FISH, or shellfish. We also recommend using it to dress grilled vegetables and salads.

MAKES ABOUT 2 CUPS (500 ML)

1/2 cup (125 ml) freshly squeezed lemon juice
  (3 to 4 lemons)

1 teaspoon grated lemon zest

2 tablespoons tarragon vinegar

1 tablespoon finely minced shallot

2 teaspoons dried tarragon

2 teaspoons amber-colored honey,
  such as clover or wildflower

1/2 cup (125 ml) olive oil

1/4 cup (50 ml) chicken broth

Fine kosher or sea salt and
  ground white pepper

In a medium-size bowl, mix together the lemon juice, zest, vinegar, shallot, tarragon, and honey. Whisk in the olive oil and broth and season with salt and white pepper. The vinaigrette will not emulsify. Use immediately or pour into a medium-size jar with a tight-fitting lid. It will keep in the refrigerator for up to 3 days.

FOUR-HERB PISTOU

A TRADITIONAL FRENCH *PISTOU* IS MADE WITH FRESH BASIL, GARLIC, AND OLIVE oil but no pine nuts (as in Italian pesto). The addition of chives and mint or lemon balm keeps the pistou a brilliant grassy green. Pistou turns into a luscious marinade when mixed with several tablespoons of oil and vinegar.

MAKES 2 CUPS (500 ML)

3 garlic cloves, roughly chopped

½ cup (125 ml) packed fresh flat-leaf parsley

½ cup (125 ml) fresh basil

½ cup (125 ml) packed fresh mint
   or lemon balm

½ cup (125 ml) snipped chives or garlic chives

½ cup (125 ml) extra-virgin olive oil

⅓ cup (75 ml) freshly grated Parmesan
   or Romano cheese

Kosher salt and freshly ground black pepper

In a food processor, pulse garlic, parsley, basil, mint, and chives until finely chopped. With the motor running, through the feed tube, gradually add the olive oil. Add the cheese and pulse until you have a coarse-grained green sauce. Season with salt and pepper.

Store in an airtight container in the refrigerator for up to 2 weeks or in the freezer for up to 6 months.

HERBES DE PROVENCE FLAVORING PASTE

GIVE YOUR GRILLED AND SMOKED FOODS A TRUE SOUTH-OF-FRANCE FLAIR WHEN YOU slather fish, lamb, pork, game, or chicken with this bold mixture. If you don't have lavender buds, substitute dried rosemary.

MAKES ABOUT 1/2 CUP (125 ML)

2 garlic cloves, minced

1/4 cup (50 ml) Dijon mustard

1/4 cup (50 ml) olive oil

2 teaspoons dried herbes de Provence

1/2 teaspoon dried lavender buds
(culinary use only)

Kosher salt or sea salt and
freshly ground black pepper

In a bowl, combine the garlic, mustard, olive oil, herbes de Provence, and lavender. Season with salt and pepper. Store in an airtight container in the refrigerator for up to 3 days.

DIJON MUSTARD–MAYONNAISE SLATHER

THIS IS A GREAT SLATHER ON SALMON OR ANY OTHER FISH FOR PLANKING. IT IS also a great dipping sauce for grilled asparagus or artichokes. The aioli recipes can also be used as slathers.

MAKES 1 CUP (250 ML)

1/2 cup (125 ml) mayonnaise

1/2 cup (125 ml) Dijon mustard

In a bowl, whisk together the mayonnaise and mustard. Store in an airtight container in the refrigerator for up to 1 week.

VARIATIONS:

Artichoke Slather: Finely chop 5 or 6 canned artichoke hearts and add to slather.

Shallot Slather: Finely chop 3 or 4 shallots and add to slather.

Caper Slather: Finely chop 3 or 4 tablespoons of drained capers and add to slather.

Artichoke-Shallot-Caper Slather: Add 2 finely chopped tablespoons of each.

FOOD PROCESSOR AIOLI

AIOLI IS A GARLICKY MAYONNAISE FROM PROVENCE USED TO ACCOMPANY FISH AND shellfish, but we love it with grilled salmon or a platter of grilled vegetables. The trick to making light, fluffy aioli in a food processor is using the whole egg instead of just egg yolks. If the food safety of raw eggs is a concern for you, use pasteurized eggs in their shells or ½ cup (125 ml) pasteurized liquid whole egg.

MAKES ABOUT 2 CUPS (500 ML)

2 large eggs

2 to 4 garlic cloves, minced

1 tablespoon freshly squeezed lemon juice

1 tablespoon Dijon mustard

1½ cups (375 ml) olive oil

In a food processor, combine the eggs, garlic, lemon juice, and mustard; pulse to blend. With the motor running, through the food tube, gradually add the olive oil, processing until thick and creamy. Store in an airtight container in the refrigerator for up to 3 days.

VARIATIONS:

Smoked Garlic Aioli: Use 2 to 4 smoked garlic cloves instead. To smoke garlic, leave the cloves whole with the skin on, brush with olive oil and place in a foil pan. Prepare an indirect fire with a kiss of smoke in your grill (page 15), using three wood chunks, such as apple, cherry, hickory, oak, or pecan. Place the chunks of wood directly on the ashed-over charcoal or a handful of flavored wood chips or wood pellets in a foil packet (with holes punched in it so the smoke can escape) on a gas grill near a burner. Place the foil pan on the indirect side of the grill, close the lid and smoke for 2 hours. Smoked garlic keeps in the refrigerator for several days or in the freezer for 1 month.

For a wonderfully herb-fragrant twist, add 1 to 2 tablespoons of a fresh herb such as basil, chives, or tarragon to the aioli.

THE *BBQ BISTRO* SMOKE PANTRY

A little smoke flavor provides the flavor of hearth cooking, harking back to the days before *haute cuisine*. A smoky ingredient, like bacon in *boeuf bourguignon*, adds depth to a dish. But that smoky ingredient doesn't have to be meat. Vegetables can do just as well.

When you're smoking vegetables for another dish, smoke extra for leftovers (*les restes*) and then freeze them for later use. You'll need to prepare a hot fire on one side of your grill for indirect cooking and have wood chips or chunks smoldering (see page 15 for kiss of smoke). Simply brush prepared vegetables with olive oil, season, then place them in a disposable aluminum pan on the indirect (or no-heat) side of the grill. Cover and smoke until the vegetables have softened and have a good smoky aroma and a burnished appearance. Let cool, then chop if you like, and place in freezer containers, marking the date, quantity, and type of vegetable. When you want to use them, simply thaw and use on sandwiches or in soups, pastas, or sauces. If you like, use the stovetop smoker (see page 72 for how to use it) to smoke smaller quantities of vegetables.

Here are specific techniques for French garden vegetables:

BELL PEPPERS. Smoke whole peppers—especially red bell peppers, or *poivrons rouge*—then quarter, stem, seed, and freeze.

GARLIC. Peel and thread whole cloves of *ail* onto skewers. Or smoke a whole garlic bulb until soft, then squeeze out smoked garlic cloves and remove papery covering. Freeze softened garlic cloves.

ONIONS. Smoke whole, round *oignons*. Trim and chop grilled onions and freeze.

TOMATOES. Smoke whole *tomates* until softened, then peel and seed before freezing.

WINTER SQUASH OR PUMPKIN. Cut in half or quarter and scoop out seeds. Brush cut sides with olive oil, season, and place cut-side down in the pan. Scoop out softened, smoked *courge musquée* or *citrouille* and freeze.

WHITE TRUFFLE AIOLI

W E LOVE THIS AIOLI WITH GRILLED OR SMOKED BEEF TENDERLOIN, GRILLED potatoes, or grilled seafood, especially tuna. White truffle oil is available at gourmet shops or online. It has an earthy fragrance, and a few drops added to mashed potatoes or risotto is delicious. This recipe contains raw egg yolks. If the food safety of raw eggs is a concern for you, use pasteurized eggs. Many grocery stores now carry pasteurized eggs in their shells. Alternatively, use ¼ cup (50 ml) pasteurized liquid whole egg; the aioli won't be quite as rich.

MAKES ABOUT 1½ CUPS (375 ML)

2 egg yolks

1 large garlic clove, minced

1 teaspoon freshly squeezed lemon juice

¼ teaspoon kosher salt

¼ teaspoon freshly ground white pepper

1 cup (250 ml) olive oil

1 to 2 tablespoons white truffle oil

In a glass bowl, whisk together the egg yolks, garlic, lemon juice, salt, and white pepper until smooth. Gradually whisk in the olive oil and truffle oil until the sauce thickens. Store in an airtight container in the refrigerator for up to 3 days.

LIME-CILANTRO REMOULADE

REMOULADE, AN HERB MAYONNAISE, IS A CLASSIC SAUCE WITH FISH AND SHELL-fish, but this version gives it red-carpet style. It's particularly good with grilled tuna. If the food safety of raw eggs is a concern for you, use pasteurized eggs. Many grocery stores now carry pasteurized eggs in their shells. Alternatively, use ¼ cup (50 ml) pasteurized liquid whole egg.

MAKES ABOUT 1½ CUPS (375 ML)

2 tablespoons finely chopped cilantro leaves

1 teaspoon grated onion

2 large hard-boiled egg yolks

1 teaspoon anchovy paste

1 garlic clove, minced

1 large egg

1 cup (250 ml) extra-virgin olive oil

½ teaspoon lime zest

Juice of 1 lime

Place the cilantro, onion, egg yolks, anchovy paste, garlic, and whole egg in a food processor or blender and process into a paste. With the motor running, through the food tube, gradually add the olive oil, processing until thick and creamy. Stir in the lime zest and juice. Cover tightly and chill until ready to serve. You can make the remoulade up to 24 hours in advance. Store in an airtight container in the refrigerator for up to 3 days.

SAUCE *RAPIDE*

Another bistro version of a quick, stir-together sauce is one made with crème fraîche. You can buy crème fraîche in the dairy section of better grocery stores or make your own by stirring equal parts of heavy whipping cream into dairy sour cream and letting it sit at room temperature for a few hours. A little mashed avocado and lime juice take crème fraîche in a savory direction for grilled vegetables, fish, shellfish, chicken, and lamb. A little brown sugar and rum take it in a sweet direction for grilled fruit.

AVOCADO CRÈME FRAÎCHE

Makes about 1½ cups (340 g)

1 small, ripe avocado, pitted

1 cup (226 g) crème fraîche or sour cream

2 to 3 tablespoons freshly squeezed lime juice

½ teaspoon granulated sugar

Kosher salt

Spoon the avocado pulp into a small bowl and mash until smooth with a fork. Add crème fraîche, lime juice, sugar, and salt to taste; fold together. Refrigerate for a least 1 hour, covered, or until thick. Store in an airtight container in the refrigerator for up to 2 days.

BROWN SUGAR CRÈME FRAÎCHE

Makes about 1½ cups (340 g)

1 cup (226 g) crème fraîche or sour cream

2 to 3 tablespoons rum

2 to 3 tablespoons packed dark brown sugar

Mix the crème fraîche, rum, and brown sugar together in a bowl. Refrigerate for at least 1 hour, covered, or until thick. Store in an airtight container in the refrigerator for up to 4 days.

LEMON-TARRAGON CREAM SAUCE

THIS LUSCIOUS SAUCE TASTES WONDERFUL WITH SMOKED CHICKEN, TURKEY, OR LAMB. It is perfect to serve with asparagus, broccoli, cauliflower, and green beans, too.

MAKES ABOUT 2$\frac{1}{2}$ CUPS (625 ML)

1 tablespoon unsalted butter

2 tablespoons finely chopped shallots

2 tablespoons tarragon vinegar

1 tablespoon cracked black peppercorns

1 cup (250 ml) dry white wine

1 cup (250 ml) chicken stock

1 cup (250 ml) heavy whipping cream

Grated zest and juice of 2 lemons

1 teaspoon chopped fresh tarragon

Kosher salt

In a saucepan, melt the butter over medium heat. Sauté the shallots until tender, then add the vinegar, pepper, wine, and chicken stock; increase heat and bring to a boil. Reduce the heat to medium and simmer for 10 minutes, or until the mixture has reduced by about a third.

Add the cream, lemon zest, and lemon juice; simmer, stirring occasionally, for 10 minutes, until slightly thickened. Stir in the tarragon and salt to taste. Store in an airtight container in the refrigerator for up to 3 days. Reheat gently.

WHOLE-GRAIN MUSTARD SAUCE

THIS IS A DELICIOUS SAUCE TO SERVE WITH GRILLED FISH, POULTRY, AND VEGETAbles. This sauce can also be used as a slather for planked fish, pork, or chicken. It's an excellent sandwich spread, or use it as a smear on tartine with fresh tomatoes.

MAKES ABOUT 1$\frac{1}{2}$ CUPS (375 ML)

$\frac{1}{2}$ cup (125 ml) Dijon mustard

$\frac{1}{2}$ cup (125 ml) whole-grain mustard

$\frac{1}{2}$ cup (125 ml) mayonnaise

1 tablespoon freshly squeezed lemon juice

1 teaspoon dried dill weed

1 teaspoon Worcestershire sauce

$\frac{1}{2}$ teaspoon freshly ground white pepper

In a bowl, whisk together the Dijon mustard, whole-grain mustard, mayonnaise, lemon juice, dill, Worcestershire sauce, and white pepper. Store in an airtight container in the refrigerator for up to 1 week.

HOLLANDAISE SAUCE

SERVE THIS WONDERFUL ALL-PURPOSE SAUCE ON GRILLED VEGETABLES, FISH, CHICKEN, or that breakfast classic—eggs Benedict. If the food safety of raw eggs is a concern for you, use pasteurized eggs. Many grocery stores now carry pasteurized eggs in their shells.

MAKES ABOUT 1½ CUPS (375 ML)

6 large egg yolks

2 tablespoons freshly squeezed lemon juice

1 teaspoon dry mustard

1 cup (226 g) unsalted butter, melted and hot

¼ teaspoon cayenne pepper
  or hot sauce, or more

Fine kosher or sea salt

Place the egg yolks, lemon juice, and mustard in a food processor or blender and process until smooth. Slowly drizzle in the hot melted butter, pulsing the food processor or with the blender on low speed, until the sauce thickens. Add the cayenne and season with salt. Keep warm in the top of a double boiler or transfer to a stainless steel bowl and set over a pan of hot, not boiling, water until ready to serve.

VARIATION:

Browned Butter Hollandaise: Melt and then keep cooking the butter until it browns. Then add it to the egg yolks in the food processor and pulse until the sauce thickens.

BÉARNAISE SAUCE

THIS IS A BOLDER VERSION OF THE CLASSIC UNDERSTATED BÉARNAISE, WHICH makes it perfect for grilled foods, from burgers and steak to artichokes, asparagus, chicken, lamb, fish, and shellfish. Emulsion sauces like this one sometimes get cranky or *excentrique* and separate—usually if you've left them on higher heat too long. If that happens, don't despair. Remove the sauce from the heat and gently whisk in a small ice cube, and all should be well—and smooth—again.

MAKES ABOUT 1 CUP (250 ML)

⅓ cup (75 ml) dry white wine

¼ cup (50 ml) tarragon vinegar

1 tablespoon finely chopped shallot

1 teaspoon dried tarragon

¼ teaspoon fine kosher or sea salt

¾ cup (170 g) unsalted butter, cut into pieces

3 large egg yolks, lightly beaten

Cayenne pepper or hot sauce

Additional dried tarragon (optional)

In a small saucepan, bring wine, vinegar, shallot, tarragon, and salt to a boil over high heat. Boil until reduced to about 2 tablespoons, about 8 minutes. Reduce heat to low and whisk in butter, one piece at a time, until melted. Whisk in egg yolks and cook, whisking constantly, for 4 to 5 minutes, or until slightly thickened.

Remove from heat and whisk in pepper to taste. Whisk in more tarragon, if desired.

VARIATION:

Sauce Paloise: Substitute white wine vinegar for the tarragon vinegar and dried mint for the tarragon.

THE BISTRO GRILL PANTRY

What is the French term for shortcut? *Raccourci,* if you please. That's just what grilled vegetables give you, and a stylish shortcut at that. Garden vegetables are ideal to grill, cool, then chop if you like and place in freezer containers, marking the date, quantity, and type of vegetable. When you want to use them, simply thaw and then use on sandwiches or in soups, tartines, or salads.

Simply brush prepared vegetables with olive oil, season, and then grill over a medium-hot fire until they have good grill marks.

Here are specific techniques for favorite French garden vegetables:

ASPARAGUS. Chop grilled spears of *asperge* and freeze.

BELL PEPPERS. Grill whole peppers—especially red peppers or *poivrons rouge*—then quarter, stem, seed, and freeze.

EGGPLANT. Cut *aubergine* into 1-inch-thick (2.5 cm) horizontal slices to grill. Leave as slices or chop and then freeze.

LEEKS. Grill baby leeks whole; slice larger *poireaux* lengthwise and grill.

ONIONS. Grill green or bulb *oignons* whole; grill round onions in slices. Chop grilled onions and freeze.

YELLOW SUMMER SQUASH OR ZUCCHINI. Cut *courgettes* into 1-inch-thick (2.5 cm) horizontal slices to grill. Leave as slices or chop and then freeze.

MUSTARD-CORNICHON BEURRE BLANC

SIMILAR IN PIQUANT FLAVOR TO BÉARNAISE, THIS BEURRE BLANC IS EASY TO MAKE, and it's a great way to use up that odd jar of cornichons (small, whole pickled cucumbers) left over from the last time you served pâté. We love the sauce on grilled lamb, beef, chicken, fish, or vegetables. To keep the sauce warm, place the saucepan over a larger saucepan of hot water for up to 30 minutes.

MAKES 1½ CUPS (375 ML)

½ cup (113 g) unsalted butter, softened

⅓ cup (75 ml) Dijon mustard

1 shallot, minced

1 cup (250 ml) dry white wine

⅓ cup (75 ml) tarragon vinegar

12 cornichons, finely chopped (about ½ cup/125 ml)

⅓ cup (75 ml) heavy whipping cream

2 tablespoons minced fresh tarragon

Kosher salt and finely ground black pepper

In a small bowl, mash the butter and mustard until well blended. Cover and refrigerate for 15 minutes. In a small saucepan, bring shallot, wine, and vinegar to a boil over high heat. Boil until reduced by about two-thirds, about 10 minutes. Reduce heat to medium and whisk in butter mixture, 1 tablespoon at a time, until all the butter has been incorporated and the sauce has thickened slightly. Remove from heat and whisk in cornichons, cream, and tarragon. Season with salt and pepper. Serve warm.

THREE-PEPPERCORN BEURRE BLANC

S PRINKLE FOODS DESTINED FOR THE GRILL WITH THREE-PEPPERCORN RUB (PAGE 23), then serve this sauce as an accompaniment for a welcome culinary heat.

MAKES ABOUT 1 CUP (250 ML)

2 teaspoons Szechuan or white peppercorns

1 teaspoon black peppercorns

1 teaspoon dried green peppercorns

3/4 cup (175 ml) dry white wine

1 tablespoon minced shallot

1 cup (226 g) cold unsalted butter, cubed

1/4 teaspoon fine kosher or sea salt

Place all the peppercorns in a small cast-iron skillet over medium-high heat and toast, stirring frequently, until aromatic, about 2 minutes. Scrape into a mortar and grind with pestle until crushed but still somewhat coarse.

In a small saucepan, bring the crushed peppercorns, wine, and shallot to a boil. Continue to boil until reduced to 2 tablespoons, 10 to 15 minutes. Remove the pan from the heat and turn the heat to low. Whisk in 2 cubes of butter, then return the pan to the heat. Whisk until the butter has almost melted into the liquid. Continue whisking in the butter, one cube at a time, until all the butter has been emulsified into the sauce and the sauce has thickened. Remove from the heat immediately and whisk in the salt. Keep warm in the top of a double boiler or transfer to a stainless steel bowl and set over a pan of hot, not boiling, water until ready to serve.

CHAPTER 2

HORS D'OEUVRES
APPETIZERS

The French idea of an hors d'oeuvre or appetizer is something very flavorful—briny, bitter, smoky, buttery—that can be served with an aperitif (Kir, Lillet, Dubonnet, Pernod, Champagne, or a dry white or rosé wine) to stimulate the appetite.

The appetizers in this chapter fit that bill deliciously. For briny and smoky, you can't do better than Wood-Grilled Oysters with Smoky Bacon (page 43). Slightly bitter Grilled Asparagus Aioli Platter (page 50) or Grilled Baby Artichokes with Parmesan and Lemon Drizzle (page 49) can do double duty as either an appetizer or a side dish. Buttery only begins to describe the flavor of Planked Scallops with Pistachio Butter (page 45), one of the easiest and most delicious appetizers you can grill. You'll love these so much that you may want to double the recipe and serve the scallops as your main course next time.

An appetizer portion is small, and a little goes a long way, so you can also splurge a bit on ingredients, whether you select the freshest shellfish or Grilled Foie Gras de Moulard (page 51) to sizzle and serve.

PAN-GRILLED MUSSELS

MOULES MARINIÈRE, THAT CLASSIC BISTRO DISH, TAKES A DELICIOUS TURN WHEN mussels or clams are grill-roasted in a preheated cast-iron skillet to pop their shells. Then a deliciously simple sauce of wine, garlic, butter, and lemon juice bathes the bivalves for a few minutes until the sauce is bubbly and warm. Crusty bread for dipping into the broth is a must.

SERVES 4 TO 6

1½ pounds (750 g) mussels (about 2 dozen)

2 cups (500 ml) dry white wine

2 tablespoons unsalted butter

4 garlic cloves, minced

1 lemon, cut in half

1 loaf of rustic country bread, sliced

Prepare a hot fire in your grill. Set a large cast-iron skillet over the fire and let it heat, with the grill lid closed, for 20 minutes.

Clean the mussels under cold running water, scraping away the fibrous bits and discarding any that have broken shells or shells that won't close.

Combine the wine, butter, garlic, juice of ½ lemon, and the squeezed lemon half in a bowl to take out to the grill.

When the skillet is very hot, use grill tongs to place a single layer of mussels in the skillet, close the grill lid, and let the mussels grill-roast for about 1 minute. Open the grill lid. Some of the mussels will have begun to open. Carefully pour the wine mixture into the pan and let it to come to a boil. Close the grill lid again and grill-roast for about 3 or 4 minutes or until the mussels have all popped open. Using heavy-duty grill mitts, carefully remove the skillet to a heatproof surface. Grill slices of the bread until lightly browned on both sides, about 2 minutes per side.

To serve, discard any mussels that have not opened. Pour the broth with the mussels into a large serving bowl. Squeeze the other half of the lemon over the mussels and serve with the grilled bread.

WOOD-GRILLED OYSTERS WITH SMOKY BACON

W ITH A CRISP WHITE WINE, NOTHING'S FINER THAN THESE WOOD-GRILLED oysters garnished with a bit of bacon and served with a dollop of Food Processor Aioli (page 29) or Hollandaise Sauce (page 35). Another option for an extra punch of flavor is a small spoonful of a Compound Butter *à la Française* (page 47), your choice.

SERVES 6 TO 8

Suggested wood: Almond, apple, cherry, oak, or pecan

4 thin slices smoky bacon, cooked crisp and crumbled

36 fresh oysters on the half shell

1 cup (250 ml) Food Processor Aioli (page 29), prepared

Prepare a hot fire with a kiss of smoke (page 15) in your grill and add your desired type of wood.

Arrange the oysters on baking sheets and top each with a teaspoon of aioli and a sprinkle of bacon bits, reserving the remaining aioli.

When you see the first wisp of smoke from the wood, transfer the oysters to the grill, using grill tongs. Close the lid and grill for 3 to 5 minutes, or until the edges of the oysters begin to curl. (For very large oysters, allow a few minutes more, but don't overcook.) Serve the oysters with the reserved aioli.

AMUSE-BOUCHE

If it is just a taste that you want to serve, then that's an amuse-bouche, a single bite-size hors d'oeuvre to "amuse the mouth." All of the recipes in this chapter are perfect for plating as a single bite, with an added artful flourish. You'll want the plate to be eye-catching, so a drizzle of pale green extra-virgin olive oil plus a sauce and herbs or a frill of micro-greens for garnish should provide just the right touch.

PLANKED SCALLOPS WITH PISTACHIO BUTTER

S HOW YOUR GRILLING SAVOIR FAIRE WITH THIS EASY RECIPE THAT LOOKS AND tastes like you worked all day. Nap the scallops with the wonderful Pistachio Butter that has all the flavor of a fancy sauce, but it's no-cook! Just stir the ingredients together for a colorful and delicious compound butter that you dot over the scallops. Bread is a must for sopping everything up. Shrimp or prawns are easy to substitute for the scallops if you prefer. Other Compound Butters (page 47) can be used instead of the Pistachio Butter.

Baking planks are thicker than grilling planks and have a hollow groove carved out of the wood. This groove is perfect for holding butter or sauces on the plank versus the saucy concoctions spilling off the flat grill planks.

SERVES 6 TO 8

1 cedar or oak baking plank,
 soaked in water for at least 1 hour

Pistachio Butter

Makes about ⅔ cup (150 ml)

½ cup (125 ml) roasted, shelled pistachios

½ cup (125 g) unsalted butter,
 at room temperature

Kosher salt

1 pound (450 g) large sea scallops,
 about 16

1 loaf crusty French or Italian bread

For the Pistachio Butter, finely grind the pistachios in a food processor or by hand. Mix with the softened butter in a medium-size bowl and season with salt.

Prepare an indirect hot fire in your grill, with the fire on one side and no fire on the other.

Place the scallops on the baking plank. Dollop 1 rounded teaspoon of the Pistachio Butter onto each scallop.

Place the planked scallops on the indirect side or no-heat side of the grill. Close the lid and plank-cook until the scallops are firm and just opaque, about 20 minutes, turning the plank 180 degrees halfway through the cooking time.

Serve immediately on the planks with the remaining butter and crusty bread.

VARIATION:

Plank-Roasting in the Oven: Preheat the oven to 400°F (200°C). Place the planked scallops in the middle of the oven and close the door. Reduce the heat to 350°F (180°C) and roast for 15 to 20 minutes until the scallops are firm and just opaque.

SHRIMP GRILLED ON ROSEMARY SKEWERS

DURING THE SUMMER GRILLING SEASON YOU CAN OFTEN FIND STURDY ROSEMARY branch skewers, sold in a bundle, in fine grocery stores. Or you can buy a variety of rosemary, a plant sometimes called Tuscan Rosemary, so you can harvest branches when you need them. The easiest way to use these long rosemary branches is to strip at least half the leaves off the bottom of the branch. Save the leaves and throw them on your charcoal fire for a fragrance feast. Before you thread the shrimp onto the rosemary branch, using a thick wooden skewer, poke a hole in the middle of the shrimp to make threading them easier. This simple grilled dish reminds us of the south of France where rosemary grows abundantly in old rock walls, gravel lanes, and on the hilltops, giving passersby a whiff of that wonderful woodsy aroma.

SERVES 8

8 to 10 rosemary skewers, about 1 inch (2.5 cm) of the bottom of the sprig stripped of leaves, soaked in water for 10 minutes

½ cup (113 g) butter, melted

Juice of 2 lemons

1 pound (450 g) large shrimp, 16 to 20 count, shelled and deveined

1 lemon, cut into wedges, for garnish

Prepare a hot fire in your grill.

In a small saucepan, melt the butter with lemon juice and set aside.

Thread two shrimp onto each rosemary skewer.

Place the shrimp skewers over the hot fire and grill for 5 to 7 minutes, turning often and basting with the lemon butter.

Arrange the shrimp skewers on a platter and drizzle the remaining sauce over the skewers. Garnish with lemon wedges and serve.

COMPOUND BUTTERS
À LA FRANÇAISE

Compound butter is a butter that has at least one other ingredient added to it. These flavored butters can add panache to a dish like nothing else. They're so easy to make and, what's even better, can be *made ahead*— words that thrill any cook or barbecuer. Make up the butter, then spoon it into ramekins or roll it into a log on waxed paper or plastic wrap. Keep it in the refrigerator for up to 1 week or in the freezer for several months. Just be sure to label and date the packages so you know what you're pulling out of the freezer.

Begin with ½ cup (113 g) of unsalted butter at room temperature. Then mix in the following for the different flavored butters with a French flair.

- **PROVENÇAL BUTTER:** Add 1 tablespoon of Provençal Herb Rub (page 22) or 1 tablespoon or more of Herbes de Provence Flavoring Paste (page 28).
- **LEMON-GARLIC BUTTER:** Add 2 minced garlic cloves and the grated zest of 1 lemon.
- **FRESH HERB BUTTER:** Add 1, 2, or 3 tablespoons of finely chopped fresh herb of your choice, or a medley of fresh herbs, such as thyme, flat-leaf parsley, chives, tarragon, lavender, and rosemary, and 1 teaspoon freshly squeezed lemon juice.
- **CAPER BUTTER:** Add 1 tablespoon or more of caper paste or capers smashed with a fork.
- **TAPENADE BUTTER:** Add 1 tablespoon or more of tapenade or olive paste.
- **ANCHOVY BUTTER:** Add 1 tablespoon or more of anchovy paste.
- **SUN-DRIED TOMATO BASIL BUTTER:** Add 1 tablespoon or more of sun-dried tomato paste and ¼ cup (50 ml) freshly chopped basil.
- **PISTOU BUTTER:** Add 1 tablespoon or more of Four-Herb Pistou (page 27).
- **SHALLOT OR ONION BUTTER:** Add 6 finely chopped shallots or green onions, 1 teaspoon Worcestershire sauce, and ¼ teaspoon dry mustard.
- **RED PEPPER BUTTER:** Add 2 tablespoons or more of finely chopped red bell pepper (fire-roasted, smoked, grilled, or raw).
- **ROQUEFORT BUTTER:** Add 3 tablespoons of crumbled Roquefort blue cheese.
- **FRENCH FETA BUTTER:** Add 3 tablespoons of crumbled French feta cheese.
- **GOAT CHEESE BUTTER:** Add 3 tablespoons of softened goat cheese.
- **WHITE MISO BUTTER:** Add 1 to 2 tablespoons white miso.

GRILLED BABY ARTICHOKES
WITH PARMESAN AND LEMON DRIZZLE

WHENEVER BABY ARTICHOKES ARE AVAILABLE, GRAB THEM AND MAKE THIS dish, as tasty as it is pretty. It is important to par-cook the artichokes until they are tender before grilling them. This makes an easier job of the grilling, which simply imparts a nice char to the chokes. This is also delicious with a slight French Quarter accent by serving these with Lime-Cilantro Remoulade (page 32) in place of the Parmesan.

SERVES 4

8 baby artichokes

Grated zest and juice of 1 lemon

½ teaspoon kosher salt

1 garlic clove, minced

½ cup (125 ml) extra-virgin olive oil

¼ cup (50 ml) freshly squeezed lemon juice

Kosher salt and freshly ground black pepper

Wedge of Parmesan cheese for shaving

1 loaf good French bread, sliced

Remove the bottom outer leaves from the artichokes and trim off the stems. Slice the artichokes in half lengthwise. Trim about 1 inch (2.5 cm) off the top. Snip off the tops of the remaining outer leaves. With the tip of a teaspoon, remove the hairy chokes and discard.

Pour 2 cups (500 ml) water into a large pot and add the lemon zest, lemon juice, and salt. Bring the water to a boil and add the artichokes, cover, and cook for 5 to 6 minutes, or until artichoke bottoms are tender when pierced with a fork. Drain well and set aside.

Prepare a medium-hot fire in your grill.

In a small bowl, combine the garlic, olive oil, and lemon juice and season with salt and pepper. Brush the artichokes with some of the dressing.

Grill the artichokes for about 5 minutes, turning a couple of times, until lightly charred on all sides. Transfer to a platter and serve hot or warm with the remaining dressing drizzled over the top and a generous shaving of Parmesan cheese. Serve the sliced French bread alongside the artichoke platter to mop up the delicious dressing.

GRILLED ASPARAGUS AIOLI PLATTER

PREPARE THIS RECIPE DURING THE HEIGHT OF ASPARAGUS SEASON, FROM APRIL through June, for the most flavorful results. A thicker spear is easier to grill and dip into the aioli. Look for the most beautiful varieties—the heirloom French white *Precoce D'Argentuil*, the purple asparagus known as Purple Passion, or the green Jersey Giant or Mary Washington varieties. Trim the asparagus by snapping the bottom of the stem where there is natural give. This gets rid of the woody ends better than cutting the asparagus with a knife. White Truffle Aioli (page 31) is sensational with this dish, too.

SERVES 6 TO 8

2 pounds (1 kg) asparagus

Olive oil for brushing

1 recipe Food Processor Aioli (page 29), prepared

Prepare a medium-hot fire in your grill.

Trim the asparagus, brush with olive oil, and take out to the grill. Place the asparagus spears perpendicular to the grill rack. Grill for 8 to 10 minutes, turning often, until the asparagus is tender-crisp and has charred a bit. Transfer to a platter and serve hot or at room temperature with a bowl of the aioli for dipping.

VARIATIONS:

Instead of aioli for the asparagus, make either of these stir-together sauces when you're in a hurry. They use store-bought mayonnaise and mustard as a base and can be made several days ahead and stored in the refrigerator: Dijon Mustard–Mayonnaise Slather (page 28) or Whole-Grain Mustard Sauce (page 34).

Also, half the asparagus can be wrapped in paper-thin slices of Bayonne ham, prosciutto, or Serrano ham (or other air-dried hams) and then grilled. It makes a wonderful color contrast and adds extra flavor to the platter.

GRILLED FOIE GRAS DE MOULARD

ALWAYS A SPECIAL TREAT, FOIE GRAS IS SERVED IN BISTROS ACROSS FRANCE IN some form or another at the evening meal. For grilling you want to use the raw duck liver, not a mousse or pâté. Liver hater? Stop right there! This is the most mellow, creamy, divine flavor and silky texture that must be tasted to be believed. Specialty gourmet shops may carry foie gras or they can special order it for you. There are many reputable online sources, too. A whole lobe of liver is expensive (more than $100), but you can ask for foie gras by the slice, which will cut the cost considerably. The traditional way to prepare the foie gras is to sear it over high heat. So grilling it over high heat makes perfect sense. Serve the foie gras with a chilled Sauterne or Riesling for perfection. If you like, grill a few slices of baguette or brioche to serve with this as well.

SERVES 2 TO 4

2 slices (5 ounces/150 g) foie gras,
 ½ inch (1 cm) thick

Kosher salt and freshly ground black pepper

1 ripe pear, peeled, cored, and sliced

2 tablespoons pear or fig jam

Prepare a hot fire in your grill.

When the grill is very hot, season the foie gras with salt and pepper. Place over the fire and grill for about 1 minute per side or until golden brown with grill marks. The middle should be warm and slightly pink. Do not overcook or it will melt. To serve, plate the slices of grilled fois gras, fan the pear slices, and spoon the pear or fig jam alongside.

VARIATIONS:

Foie gras can be grilled and then refrigerated to serve as a cold appetizer. Make sure to use it within 3 days of purchase. The raw or grilled foie gras can also be frozen, but again, use it soon, within a couple of weeks.

CHAPTER 3

TARTINES & PAIN GRILLÉ
TOASTED & GRILLED BREAD

Most of us are familiar with bruschetta and crostini—toasted, open-faced bread with toppings. And that is exactly what a French tartine is. In this book, tartines get even more flavor because they are grilled over higher heat than your oven or toaster, making them sensational. Just like bruschetta, tartines can be topped with a myriad of flavorful seasonal ingredients. Ours have a French twist.

The one essential to a great tartine is the bread. The better the bread, the better the tartine. We like to use the French sandwich loaf bread known as *pain de mie*, sourdough, artisan breads of all kinds, brioche, baguettes, or any bread with a sturdy crumb and a good flavor that will stand up to the heat of the grill. Thicker-cut slices of bread will result in knife-and-fork tartines, while thinner slices can be hand held.

Tartines can start your day with Toast and Jam (page 67) or end the meal with delicious grilled fruits you'll find in our Dessert & Fruits chapter (page 200).

At Jody Williams's *gastrothèque* Buvette in New York City and Paris, softly scrambled eggs are spooned over grilled tartines, then topped with bacon or ribbons of smoked salmon. Savory tartines can be served for a brunch or lunch, like the Grilled Salmon Benedict tartine with Hollandaise (page 57). The Juicy Tomatoes and Capers tartines (page 61), as with many of the other combinations, can make a lovely light lunch or supper when served with a salad.

Pain grillé or grilled bread can be a flatbread, the crêpe-like socca, or simply bread that is slathered with olive oil and grilled to accompany another dish.

GRILLED ASPARAGUS FLATBREAD
WITH PISTACHIOS, FETA, AND LEMON AIOLI

FRENCH FLATBREADS ARE DELICIOUSLY SIMPLE. IN THE NORTH, THE ALSATIAN *tarte flambée* or *flammekuchen* is a thin flatbread made with yeast dough and topped with crème fraîche, *lardons* (bacon), and onion. In the south, *fougasse* has the filling rolled into the dough and is shaped in a leaf form. We have taken the yeast dough, rolled it thin, and then grilled it to await the French toppings of grilled asparagus, lemon aioli, feta, and pistachios. (The French feta cheese is mild and creamy and usually made from excess sheep's milk that is not used for making Roquefort.) With a flute of Champagne, life is good.

SERVES 4

1 pound (450 g) prepared pizza dough

Olive oil for brushing

1 pound (450 g) fresh asparagus

Kosher or sea salt and
   freshly ground black pepper

1 recipe Food Processor Aioli (page 29),
   prepared

4 ounces (125 g) French feta cheese, crumbled

¼ cup (30 g) shelled, roasted,
   and chopped pistachios

Prepare a medium-hot indirect fire in your grill.

Divide the dough into four parts. Pat or roll each part into a 6-inch (15-cm) oval on a floured surface. Brush both sides with olive oil and place on a baking sheet to take to the grill.

Trim the asparagus, brush with olive oil, season with salt and pepper, and take out to the grill. Place the asparagus spears perpendicular to the grill rack. Grill for 8 to 10 minutes, turning often, until the asparagus is tender-crisp and has charred a bit. Transfer to a cutting board and chop into 2-inch-long (5 cm) diagonal pieces. Set aside.

Place the dough ovals on the grill grates. Grill for 2 to 3 minutes or until the underside has good grill marks. Transfer the dough ovals to the indirect side, grilled-side up. Dollop Lemon Aioli on the top of each grilled dough oval and spread it quickly with the back of the spoon. Scatter with asparagus, and then sprinkle with feta and pistachios. Close the grill lid, and grill for 3 to 4 minutes or until the feta is beginning to melt and the dough has cooked through.

Serve warm and pass the remaining Lemon Aioli at the table.

SOCCA ON THE GRILL

ADAPTED FROM A RECIPE BY DAVID LEBOVITZ, THIS GLUTEN-FREE CHICKPEA FLATbread is street food from the south of France made even more deliciously on your grill. You can find chickpea flour at Whole Foods, health food stores, in grocery stores that carry Bob's Red Mill products, and at Indian markets as "besan" flour. This is also a great gluten-free way to entertain. Just chill out by the grill with a glass of crisp rosé and eat the socca as it comes off the grill, drizzled with olive oil or topped with accompaniments of your choice. Says Lebovitz, "Socca is meant to be in rough shards, eaten with your fingers, and is especially good after a long day on a sun-saturated beach when your skin is tingling with sand and you can lick your lips and taste the salt of the Mediterranean." Using your grill and a cast-iron skillet gives a much more authentic result.

SERVES 4

1 cup/113 g chickpea flour

1 cup (250 ml) plus 2 tablespoons water

3/4 teaspoon sea salt

1/8 teaspoon ground cumin

1 1/2 tablespoons olive oil
 plus 1 tablespoon for the pan

Kosher or sea salt and
 freshly ground black pepper

1 recipe Food Processor Aioli (page 29),
 prepared (optional)

1 cup (175 g) cured black olives (optional)

For the batter, whisk together the chickpea flour, water, salt, cumin, and 1 1/2 tablespoons of the olive oil. Let the batter rest at least 2 hours, covered and at room temperature, to slightly thicken.

Prepare a medium-hot fire in your grill. Heat a 10-inch (25-cm) cast-iron skillet on the grill grates. Close the grill lid and let the pan heat for 20 minutes.

When the grill and pan are hot, add 1 tablespoon of olive oil to the pan and pour enough batter to cover the bottom. With a grill mitt on one hand, lift the skillet and swirl the batter around to level it. Close the lid and grill for 8 minutes. Open the lid and check for doneness. Grill until the socca is firm and beginning to blister on top and burn at the edges.

To serve, slide the socca out of the pan onto a cutting board, cut or tear it into pieces, and sprinkle with salt and pepper. Serve with aioli and cured olives, if desired.

Repeat the process with the remaining socca batter, adding 1 tablespoon olive oil to the pan between each batch.

SAVORY TARTINES

So simple and so good, tartines are such an easy appetizer and a great way to use ready-made goods from the deli or *les restes* (leftovers) from your refrigerator. Make tartines really special by serving a wonderful aperitif with them.

TARTINE COMBINATIONS:

- Avocado slices or (Avocado Relish page 90) and grilled shrimp
- Smoked salmon or trout with Food Processor Aioli (page 29)
- Scrambled eggs with caviar
- Grilled Ratatouille (page 109)
- Slices of Wood-Fired Duck Breasts with Fresh Herb Butter (page 153)
- *Terrine de Campagne* (a pâté of coarsely chopped meats) with gherkins or cornichons
- Stir-Grilled Shallots with Tarragon Butter (page 106)
- Smoky Lamb Daube (page 148) with shredded Emmental cheese
- *Saucisson* (dry-cured sausage) with a smear of mustard
- Four-Herb Pistou (page 27) with toasted ground walnuts

GRILLED SALMON BENEDICT

THIS IS A GREAT WAY TO USE THE THIN TAIL END OF A SALMON FILLET TO MAKE a brunch or lunch Benedict. If you have grilled salmon from a previous meal, then this can be your déjà vu salmon Benedict, or use lox or smoked salmon from the deli. Instead of English muffins, you'll use tartines (grilled bread) as the base. We have a stir-together topping, but you could substitute Food Processor Aioli (page 29) or Hollandaise Sauce (page 35). This is a knife-and-fork tartine, rather than hand held.

SERVES 4

3 tablespoons sour cream

3 tablespoons mayonnaise

1 tablespoon lemon juice

2 tablespoons Dijon mustard

2 tablespoons snipped chives

4 slices of brioche or French bread, sliced ½ inch (1 cm) thick

Extra-virgin olive oil for brushing

4 (2-ounce/60-g) salmon fillets, about ½ inch (1 cm) thick

Kosher salt and freshly ground black pepper

4 eggs, hard-boiled and sliced

1 small (4-ounce/125-g) red onion, thinly sliced

In a small bowl, combine the sour cream, mayonnaise, lemon juice, mustard, and chives. Set aside.

Prepare a hot fire in your grill.

Lightly oil both sides of the bread. Lightly oil both sides of the salmon fillets and season with salt and pepper. Grill the bread for about 2 minutes on each side until golden brown with good grill marks. Grill the salmon for about 2½ minutes per side, turning once.

To assemble the tartines, set the toasted bread on a plate and top with the grilled salmon, a sliced hard-boiled egg, and a dollop of the sauce. Scatter the red onion slices over the top.

VARIATIONS:

For more traditional eggs Benedict, serve this dish with poached eggs over the grilled salmon or even a sunny-side-up egg on top. For a Benedict with some punch, slather the grilled bread with Four-Herb Pistou (page 27). Yum!

PROVENÇAL BUTTER AND SIZZLING MUSHROOMS

SO SIMPLE. SO GOOD.

SERVES 4

1 pound (450 g) baby bella mushrooms, sliced

Olive oil for drizzling

1 recipe Provençal Butter (page 47)

12 slices of grilled baguette

Prepare a hot fire in your grill.

Set the mushrooms in a grill wok or basket on top of a baking sheet. Lightly drizzle the mushrooms with olive oil and place over the hot fire immediately. Grill for about 5 minutes tossing the mushrooms occasionally. Set the grilled mushrooms in a bowl and top with a couple of pats of the Provençal Butter. Toss to lightly coat the mushrooms.

To serve, place the grilled bread on a platter with a small bowl of the Provençal Butter along with the larger bowl of mushrooms. Slather the toast with butter and top with mushrooms.

BLACK OLIVE TAPENADE TARTINES

TAPENADE IS A STAPLE OLIVE PASTE OF THE SOUTHERN FRENCH PANTRY. IT IS RICH, delicious, and ours has an ample amount of lemony flavor.

SERVES 4

1 baguette, sliced ¼ inch (.5 cm) thick

Olive oil for brushing

Black Olive Tapenade

1 cup (175 g) finely chopped cured black olives

2 tablespoons extra-virgin olive oil

Zest and juice of 1 lemon

2 tablespoons butter, at room temperature

Prepare a hot fire in your grill.

Lightly oil both sides of the sliced baguette and grill for about 1 or 2 minutes on each side to a light golden brown. Set aside.

For the Black Olive Tapenade, combine the olives, olive oil, lemon zest, lemon juice, and butter in a bowl.

To serve, place the bowl of tapenade in the center of a platter with the grilled slices of baguette around it.

WARM GOAT CHEESE TARTINES WITH FRESH FIGS

A GOAT CHEESE TARTINE, A JUG OF WINE, AND YOU. THIS TARTINE CAN BE ENJOYED for breakfast, as a snack, or as a bistro supper with a good green salad. Fresh apricots, pears, or even the Port Cherry Sauce (page 175) would be good substitutes for the figs.

SERVES 4

1 baguette, sliced ¼ inch (.5 cm) thick

Olive oil for brushing

8 to 10 ounces (227 to 286 g) goat cheese, cut into ¼-inch-thick (0.5 g) slices

4 ripe fresh figs, sliced lengthwise (about ½ pound/250 g)

Kosher or sea salt and freshly ground black pepper

8 sprigs or more of edible flowers like chive blossoms, nasturtium, or violets

Prepare a hot indirect fire in your grill.

Lightly oil both sides of the sliced baguette and grill for about 1 or 2 minutes on each side to a light golden brown. Place the slices of grilled baguettes in a foil pan. Place a round of the goat cheese on each toast and top with a slice of fig. Set on the indirect side of the grill and close the lid. Grill for about 5 minutes until cheese has begun to melt.

To serve, set the tartines on a platter and lightly sprinkle with salt and pepper. Scatter the edible flowers on the plate and enjoy your small feast.

HAM AND GRUYÈRE TARTINES

PATRICIA WELLS'S COOKBOOKS ARE AMONG THE MOST PRIZED IN OUR COLLECTIONS. We've each traveled and cooked from her *Food Lover's Guide to Paris*. Our cookbook club has reveled in her *Bistro Cooking*, our copies autographed from when she visited Kansas City many years ago. Her *French Kitchen Cookbook* is a delight; we have adapted her Ham and Cheese Squares with Cornichons to our open-faced version as a tartine.

SERVES 4

2 large sandwich-size pieces of brioche, sliced ½ inch (1 cm) thick

Olive oil for brushing

4 tablespoons Sun-Dried Tomato Basil Butter (page 47), prepared

8 thin slices good quality ham

8 ounces (250 g) freshly grated Gruyère or Comté cheese

8 cornichons

Prepare a hot indirect fire in your grill.

Lightly oil both sides of the sliced brioche and grill for about 1 or 2 minutes on each side to a light golden brown. Generously butter each slice of brioche with the Sun-Dried Tomato Basil Butter. Place the slices of grilled brioche in a foil pan, butter-side up. Place two pieces of ham on each slice of bread and top each piece with 4 ounces (125 g) of the grated cheese. Set on the indirect side of the grill and close the lid. Grill for about 5 minutes until cheese has begun to melt.

To serve, slice the brioche into four serving pieces either square or on the diagonal. Place a cornichon on top of each tartine with a colorful toothpick.

TRIO OF SUMMER TARTINES

If it were up to us, we'd just say Tartine de Tomate and be done with it. Nothing tastes better than a fresh, sun-ripened tomato picked from the vine and popped in your mouth—unless it is an oh-so-ripe tomato served on a fire-grilled slice of bakery bread. Well, maybe a garlic-rubbed toast with Sun Gold tomatoes squished between your fingers so all the juice is caught by the bread, and maybe a dollop of Four-Herb Pistou (page 27) or a slather of Roquefort Butter (page 47) topped with a thick slice of the reddest juiciest beefsteak tomato eaten over the sink.

JUICY TOMATOES AND CAPERS

THE BEST! USE THIS SIMPLE RECIPE AND ADD CHOPPED RED ONIONS, SNIPPED CHIVES, or torn basil for additional summer flavor.

SERVES 4

2 large beefsteak tomatoes (1 pound/500 g), chopped, saving the juices

3 tablespoons small capers, or more to taste

2 tablespoons extra-virgin olive oil

Kosher salt and freshly ground black pepper

4 large slices of grilled country bread or *pain de mie*

Combine the tomatoes and their juices, capers, and olive oil. Season with salt and pepper. Let the mixture sit for 15 minutes or more before serving on the crusty tartines.

FRENCH FETA AND CHARENTAIS MELON

SIMILAR TO CANTALOUPE, CHARENTAIS MELONS ARE SMALL WITH A DEEP ORANGE color and a highly fragrant tropical fruit and floral aroma. Sometimes you see them at specialty markets; you can also grow your own. Add some slices of dry-cured ham to the plate to serve along with this tartine, delicious for breakfast or as a light dinner with a glass of chilled rosé.

SERVES 6

1 (1-pound/500-g) ripe Charentais melon (or cantaloupe)

8 ounces (225 g) French feta cheese or goat cheese, crumbled

12 to 18 slices of grilled baguette

Cut the melon in half and remove the seeds. Slice the melon halves into six wedges and cut off the rind. Place the melon slices on a platter with a bowl of the crumbled feta in the center. Serve with a basket of the grilled tartines. Place a slice of melon on a tartine and top with some of the crumbled feta cheese.

FROMAGE BLANC AND LEMON VERBENA PISTOU

FROMAGE BLANC IS SIMILAR TO NEUFCHÂTEL CREAM CHEESE. IT'S A SOFT CREAMY spreadable cheese. It marries well with this flavorful pistou or the Four-Herb Pistou (page 27). Ricotta would be a good cheese substitute.

SERVES 6

12 to 18 slices of grilled baguette

8 ounces (225 g) fromage blanc or Neufchâtel cream cheese

1 cup (250 ml) Lemon Verbena Pistou (page 101), prepared

Fresh herbs, for garnish

Arrange the grilled tartines on a platter with a bowl each of the cheese and the pistou. Garnish with herbs. Spread the pistou onto a slice of grilled bread and top with some of the crumbled cheese.

TRIO OF AUTUMN TARTINES

<small>⸻⸻⸻⸻ ✦ ⸻⸻⸻⸻</small>

Once farm stand or homegrown tomatoes are no longer available, then it's time to switch to some autumnal offerings. It's apple, pear, and quince season. Winter squash, including pumpkins, and other vegetables cooked or grilled to make a soft spread are delicious toppings on a tartine. Cauliflower or eggplant gratin, ratatouille, pickled beets with a smear of goat cheese, sharp cheddar with thinly shaved celery, and even grilled carrot ribbons are both tasty and eye-appealing choices for toppings and garnish.

ROQUEFORT AND FRENCH BUTTER PEARS

For us, the juicy pear takes over for the summer tomato. The pear can be grilled, but if it is oh-so-juicy, then fresh slices are the way to prepare this, and one pear just isn't enough. The French butter pears are a relative of the Anjou pear (so buy Anjous if you can't find the other). They are wonderfully juicy and have just a hint of lemon.

SERVES 4

2 ripe French butter pears (8 ounces/250 g), cored and sliced

4 large slices of grilled brioche, cut in half

8 ounces (250 g) Roquefort cheese

Honey (optional)

Arrange the sliced pears on one side of a platter and the brioche tartines on the other side with a wedge of the Roquefort cheese in the middle. Serve with honey for drizzling, if desired.

TENDERLOIN AND SHAVED PARMESAN

THIS IS A MUST-HAVE TARTINE WHEN YOU HAVE LEFTOVER (*LES RESTES*) BEEF tenderloin or filet mignon; see our recipes in the Beef chapter (page 160). A shaving of just about any cheese would be compatible with the beef so try this with Gruyère, French feta, Comté, even Raclette.

SERVES 4

4 ounces (125 g) grilled beef tenderloin, sliced thin or thick

4 slices of grilled sourdough bread

4 ounces (125 g) wedge of Parmesan

To make the tartines, place slice(s) of the grilled beef tenderloin on top of the grilled bread and shave plenty of Parmesan cheese over the top.

FRENCH GARDEN RADISH TARTINES

FRESH-PICKED SPRING AND AUTUMN RADISHES SERVED WITH UNSALTED BUTTER and coarse sea salt are a classic French dish. In our book *The Gardener & the Grill*, we included a recipe for French Garden Radish Plate with Grilled Onion Butter for our "grilled" spin on the recipe. In this version, we grill the tartines and butter them with Fresh Herb Butter, Shallot or Onion Butter, or French Feta Butter (page 47). For a flavor more like Alsace-Lorraine, use a sour rye; to go more Parisian, try a baguette.

SERVES 6 TO 8

1 small loaf sour rye or a baguette, sliced ¼ inch (.5 cm) thick

Olive oil for brushing

1 recipe Fresh Herb Butter, Shallot or Onion Butter, or French Feta Butter (page 47), prepared

1 to 2 bunches (6 to 12 ounces/175 to 375 g) of small breakfast radishes, trimmed

Kosher salt or fleur de sel

Prepare a hot fire in your grill.

Lightly oil both sides of the bread and grill for about 1 or 2 minutes per side until golden brown with grill marks. Set aside.

When the tartines have cooled, lightly butter them and set on a platter.

Thinly slice the radishes with a sharp knife or a mandoline and arrange on top of the buttered tartine, sprinkle with salt, and serve.

TOAST AND JAM

Before the advent of wood stoves and then gas ranges, people used long forks to toast bread over the hearth fire. What we gained in convenience when the electric toaster came on the scene, we sacrificed in high-heat flavor. Bread starts to toast at 310°F (154°C), but it's the high heat of a grill that can produce those wonderful charry bits that add a slight touch of bitterness and smoky flavor—which is a perfect foil for a sweet jam. Look for specialty French butter—the slightly tangy Beurre Echire, voluptuous Beurre d'Isigny, or creamy Plugra—at better grocery stores or gourmet shops. Savory and sweet contrasts are in many of the following suggestions. Try the Homemade Refrigerator Jam (page 210) or any good jar of jam or preserves like Bonne Maman for a superb topping. One of their newest flavors is Golden Plum Mirabelle made from yellow plums grown in the Lorraine region of France. We paired it with the earthy flavor of rye bread.

- Grilled slices of French country bread, French butter, peach preserves, and a sprinkling of sea salt
- Grilled slices of *pain de mie*, French butter, cinnamon, and sugar
- Grilled slices of eight-grain bread with fromage blanc, chopped pistachios, and lavender honey
- Grilled slices of sourdough with fig jam, Brie, and ham
- Grilled slices of rustic rye bread with goat cheese and Bonne Maman Golden Plum Mirabelle preserves
- Grilled slices cinnamon-raisin bread with Nutella and fresh pear slices
- Grilled slices of walnut bread with cream cheese and cranberry sauce
- Grilled slices of cranberry-walnut bread with almond butter, honey, and sea salt
- Grilled slices of apricot bread with French feta cheese and honey

SALADE
SALAD

While a simple salad is more traditionally served as sort of a palate cleanser after the main course of a French meal, bistros do it differently. In these casual restaurants, salads can be in the realm of vegetable-based first courses—think of the famous grated vegetable bistro salads. They can also be simpler green salads served with some kind of cheese after the main course. The third type of salad is the *salade composèe*, or what we would think of as a main course salad, attractively arranged.

We have all types of bistro salads in this chapter. For the vegetable first course–type of salad, you can't go wrong with Haricots Verts Salad with Mustard-Shallot Vinaigrette (page 70), one that we learned to make after trips to France. Celery Root Remoulade (page 71) and Bistro Grated Carrot Salad (page 73) also fall, deliciously, into this category.

Simpler green salads—with or without grilled greens—get a little extra flavor from smoked goat cheese, feta, or Roquefort. Try Smoked Goat Cheese Salad with Sweet Cherries (page 77), Grilled Endive with French Feta and Walnut Vinaigrette (page 75), and Char-Grilled Romaine, Bacon, Tomato, and Roquefort (page 74).

Grilling greens adds flavor through caramelization. The best greens to grill include romaine, cabbage, endive, and chard. Grill the greens, cut sides brushed with olive oil, directly on the grill grates, with the grill lid up so the greens caramelize but don't steam and wilt.

The last type of salad is the *salade composèe*, most notably the Grilled Tuna Niçoise with Lime-Cilantro Remoulade (page 81).

With salads this delicious, you may decide that a baguette and a *verre de vin* are all you need for a satisfying meal.

HARICOTS VERTS SALAD
WITH MUSTARD-SHALLOT VINAIGRETTE

HARICOTS VERTS ARE THOSE TINY, THIN FRENCH GREEN BEANS THAT START TO come on the market in late spring. They are also easy to grow in the garden. These beans should be cooked until just slightly crunchy, and then dressed warm with the vinaigrette. Use a lighter olive oil, not extra-virgin, as you don't want the olive oil flavor to dominate here.

SERVES 4

1 pound (450 g) haricots verts
or young, thin green beans

Mustard-Shallot Vinaigrette

1 large (1.5 ounce/45 g) shallot, diced

1 tablespoon Dijon mustard

1/4 cup (50 ml) white wine vinegar

1/2 cup (125 ml) olive oil

Fine kosher or sea salt and
freshly ground black pepper

Put the beans in a large pot with enough water to cover them. Bring to a boil and cook until crisp-tender, 1 to 2 minutes. Drain in a colander and rinse under cold running water for 30 seconds to refresh the color but still keep them slightly warm. Let drain for 1 minute, and then transfer to a serving bowl.

To make the vinaigrette, whisk the shallot, mustard, and vinegar together in a small bowl. Slowly drizzle in the olive oil, whisking to blend. Season with the salt and pepper. Pour the vinaigrette over the beans, toss to coat, and serve immediately.

SIMPLE BISTRO SALADS À DEUX

To make a simple Garden Tomato Salad for two, cut two medium-size tomatoes into wedges. Season with kosher or sea salt and freshly ground pepper. Lightly drizzle with extra-virgin olive oil or Lemon-Tarragon Vinaigrette (page 26) and let sit for a few minutes before serving.

To make a simple Green Salad for two, wash, dry, and tear the freshest greens you can find at the market or from your garden, about two handfuls. Place in a bowl, and when ready to eat, lightly toss with 1 tablespoon of Walnut Oil Vinaigrette (page 26) or the vinaigrette of your choice.

CELERY ROOT REMOULADE

KNOBBY, ROUND CELERY ROOT DOESN'T LOOK LIKE MUCH IN THE PRODUCE AISLE, but appearances can be deceiving. Celery root, with its gentle flavor halfway between celery and potato, transforms into creamy soups and this grated salad, a bistro staple. True Parisian remoulade is mustard-based, not like New Orleans–style remoulade, which is more like tartar sauce. This recipe is adapted from one by well-known cookbook author and Francophile Patricia Wells, our American friend in Paris. For this salad, you simply toss the grated celery root in the Remoulade dressing for a delicious accompaniment to grilled anything. Cut celery root can turn dark, like potatoes, so make quick work of grating them and toss them in the dressing *tout suite*.

SERVES 4 TO 6

Remoulade

½ cup (125 ml) mayonnaise

¼ cup (55 ml) sour cream

¼ cup (55 ml) heavy whipping cream

2 tablespoons freshly squeezed lemon juice

2 tablespoons Dijon mustard

2 teaspoons minced flat-leaf parsley

4 green onions, chopped

Coarse kosher or sea salt and
    freshly ground black pepper

1 (1-pound/500-g) celery root

For the Remoulade, whisk the mayonnaise, sour cream, and heavy whipping cream together in a bowl until smooth. Whisk in the lemon juice, mustard, and parsley and then add the green onions. Season with the salt and pepper. Set aside.

Peel and quarter the celery root, then grate in a food processor or by hand on the large holes of a box grater. As you grate each quarter, transfer it to the dressing in the bowl and stir to coat. This keeps the celery root from darkening. Serve at room temperature or chilled.

STOVETOP SMOKING *RAPIDE*

A stovetop smoker does just what its title suggests: It smokes foods indoors on your stovetop. Made of stainless steel, the stovetop smoker is designed to trap and smolder tiny wood particles away from the food so the resulting smoke permeates the food but doesn't make your kitchen smoke alarm go crazy. This gadget makes short work out of smoking goat cheese, shrimp, and tomatoes. It looks like a covered sheet cake pan.

To use the stovetop smoker, place about 1 tablespoon of very fine wood chips in the center of the base of the smoker. These chips are available in many different varieties, including apple, cherry, oak, maple, and pecan. Make sure the chips are dry when you put them in the smoker so that they will smolder effectively.

A metal drip tray fits snugly on top of the chips, then a coated, footed wire rack is placed on the tray. Coat or brush whatever food you're smoking with olive oil, then season it with salt and pepper.

Arrange your food in a single layer on the rack, so you have the most surface area exposed to the smoke. Slide the metal lid closed, extend the handles, and place the smoker over one burner. Gas or electric coil burners work just fine, but flat ceramic burners require 20 percent more cooking time. Also, make sure you have good ventilation; open a window or turn on a fan.

Turn the burner to medium (375°F/190°C) or medium-high (400°F/200°C) heat. Although the instructions enclosed with the smoker say to keep the heat on medium, we don't. We mainly use medium-high heat so that the food gets cooked fast and doesn't dry out. Your stovetop smoker won't be in perfect alignment after placing it over medium-high heat, but who cares? Ours still work just fine.

Start keeping track of the cooking time when you see the first wisp of smoke escaping from the smoker.

It's easy to tell when your food is done. Fish and shellfish should have a bronze cast and be opaque all the way through. Chicken, beef, and pork also will have a bronzish color and can be checked for doneness with an instant-read meat thermometer. Vegetables and cheeses are done when they have the amount of smoky taste you desire.

BISTRO GRATED CARROT SALAD

THIS IS SIMPLICITY ITSELF. THE FRESHEST GARDEN CARROTS MAKE ALL THE difference. Other fresh-from-the-garden vegetables that could be substituted for the carrots are finely sliced celery, halved cherry tomatoes, or thinly sliced tomatoes served on a platter and drizzled with the dressing.

SERVES 4 TO 6

4 cups finely shredded carrot, about
  6 medium-size carrots (12 ounces/375 g)
1 tablespoon freshly squeezed lemon juice
1 tablespoon olive oil

2 tablespoons tarragon or raspberry vinegar
Finely chopped fresh flat-leaf parsley,
  for garnish

Place the grated carrot in a large bowl. In a small bowl, stir together the lemon juice, olive oil, and vinegar. Drizzle the dressing over the grated carrot and toss to blend. Serve at once, garnished with parsley.

CHAR-GRILLED ROMAINE, BACON, TOMATO, AND ROQUEFORT

FRENCH BISTRO SALAD MEETS AMERICAN IN THIS FUSION DISH. YOU CAN MAKE a meal of this salad, served with crusty bread. The vinaigrette can be stored in the refrigerator for up to 2 weeks. If you love this salad, change it up by switching dressings. The Mustard-Shallot Vinaigrette (page 70) would be superb. Do not trim the core of the lettuce or several of the outer leaves will fall off.

SERVES 6

Classic Vinaigrette

¾ cup (175 ml) vegetable oil

¼ cup (50 ml) white wine vinegar

1 tablespoon granulated sugar

1 teaspoon Dijon mustard

1 teaspoon kosher salt

3 hearts of romaine, halved lengthwise, washed, and dried

Olive oil for brushing

Kosher or sea salt and freshly ground black pepper

12 strips bacon, cooked crisp and crumbled

3 cups (420 g) halved cherry tomatoes

6 ounces (175 g) Roquefort or other hearty blue cheese

For the Classic Vinaigrette, combine the oil, vinegar, sugar, mustard, and salt in a glass jar with tight-fitting lid; cover and shake to blend.

Prepare a hot fire in your grill.

Lightly brush the cut side of the romaine with olive oil and season with salt and pepper. Place the cut-side down on the grill. Grill for 3 to 4 minutes, or until outer lettuce leaves are charred and there are good grill marks on the cut side. (Do not close the grill lid or the lettuce will wilt.)

Portion the romaine among six plates and top with bacon, tomatoes, and Roquefort. Drizzle with the Classic Vinaigrette.

VARIATION:

To turn the Classic Vinaigrette into a creamy Roquefort dressing, add ½ cup (125 ml) mayonnaise and ½ cup (90 g) crumbled blue cheese; stir to blend.

GRILLED ENDIVE WITH FRENCH FETA AND WALNUT VINAIGRETTE

GRILLED GREENS ARE DELICIOUS, ALWAYS A WELCOME SURPRISE TO PEOPLE WHO have never tasted them before. They are charry on the outside and still crisp inside, blending the best of "grilled" and "salad."

SERVES 4

8 small heads Belgian endive,
    outer leaves trimmed

Olive oil for brushing

Kosher salt and freshly ground black pepper

½ cup (90 g) crumbled French feta cheese,
    like Valbreso

½ cup (125 ml) Walnut Oil Vinaigrette
    (page 26), prepared

Prepare a hot fire in your grill.

Brush the endive with olive oil. Grill for 5 to 8 minutes, turning every 2 minutes, until nicely charred.

Place the grilled endive on a platter and season lightly with salt and pepper. Top with the crumbled feta and drizzle with the vinaigrette.

SMOKED GOAT CHEESE SALAD WITH SWEET CHERRIES

LONG A FIXTURE OF BISTRO MENUS, THE WARM GOAT CHEESE SALAD FEATURED A round of goat cheese coated in breadcrumbs and baked. In *BBQ Bistro* style, the goat cheese has a noticeable smoke aroma while staying soft, warm, and creamy. A mixture of tender greens is best for this salad. To add to the butter lettuce, try mâche or the mixture of tiny lettuces known as *mesclun*. The goat cheese can also be served as a dip with crackers, toasted bread, or endive. Sweet cherries add a bright color and flavor note.

SERVES 4

Suggested wood: Apple, cherry, grapevines, orange, or oak

¼ cup (60 ml) olive oil

¼ teaspoon kosher salt

¼ teaspoon ground black pepper

⅓ cup (50 g) toasted breadcrumbs

Four 2-ounce (55-g) portions soft goat cheese

1 head butter lettuce, washed, dried, and torn

1 cup (50 g) sweet cherries, pitted

1 recipe Classic Vinaigrette (page 74), prepared

Prepare an indirect fire with a kiss of smoke (page 15) in your grill and add your desired type of wood.

In a shallow bowl, blend the olive oil, salt, and pepper. Place the breadcrumbs in a separate shallow bowl. Dip each portion of goat cheese in the olive oil and then the bread crumbs. Place the coated cheese in an aluminum pan. Set the pan on the indirect side of the grill and close the lid. Smoke the cheese for about 50 to 60 minutes.

Arrange one quarter of the lettuce on each of four plates. Set one quarter of the cherries on each plate. Top the salad with a portion of the smoked goat cheese. Then drizzle the vinaigrette over the top and serve at once.

GRILLED RED AND SAVOY CABBAGE
WITH ROQUEFORT AND CELERY SEED DRESSING

GRILLED WEDGES OF RED AND GREEN CABBAGE LOOK OH SO *RUSTIQUE* AND TASTE SO *incroyable* in this salad. If you love Roquefort cheese, add more as you like. If you don't care for Roquefort (heaven forbid) you may skip the cheese or substitute a French feta. Napa cabbage is a delicious substitute for either of the cabbages.

SERVES 8

Celery Seed Dressing

¾ cup (175 ml) vegetable oil

⅓ cup (75 ml) cider vinegar

2 tablespoons granulated sugar

1 teaspoon celery seeds

½ teaspoon kosher salt

½ teaspoon ground white pepper

¼ teaspoon dry mustard

2 garlic cloves, minced

1 small head red cabbage, quartered lengthwise

1 small head Savoy cabbage, quartered lengthwise

Olive oil for brushing

Kosher or sea salt and freshly ground pepper

8 ounces (227 g) Roquefort cheese, crumbled

For the Celery Seed Dressing, combine all of the dressing ingredients in a bowl and whisk to blend. Set aside.

Prepare a medium-hot fire in your grill.

Brush the cut sides of the cabbages with olive oil and season with salt and pepper. Grill on the cut sides of the cabbage, turning once, until browned with good grill marks and warm and supple in the middle, about 5 minutes per side. Place cabbages on a platter and drizzle with dressing and sprinkle with cheese.

GRILLED TUNA NIÇOISE
WITH LIME-CILANTRO REMOULADE

THE CLASSIC TUNA NIÇOISE—WITH COOKED BUT NOT GRILLED TUNA—HAS REMAINED a classic for a reason—it tastes refreshing in hot weather. It tastes even more so when you add the flavor of the grill. Before you grill the tuna, skewer baby Yukon potatoes and brush them with oil and season. Grill them until tender, turning often, then grill the tuna. Although the classic Tuna Niçoise features a basic vinaigrette, we think that Lime-Cilantro Remoulade keeps the French accent and is better with grilled tuna. Arrange it all on white plates into what the French call a *salade composèe* or an artful salad.

SERVES 4

1 pound (450 g) baby Yukon potatoes,
    threaded onto skewers

¼ cup (50 ml) olive oil

2 tablespoons tarragon vinegar

1 bay leaf, slightly crunched

Fine kosher or sea salt and
    freshly ground black pepper

Four 5-ounce (150-g) yellowfin tuna steaks,
    cut 1 inch (2.5 cm) thick

4 ounces (125 g) baby greens

2 large hard-boiled eggs, shelled and quartered

3 cups (420 g) cherry tomatoes

3 ounces (90 g) cured black olives

1 recipe Lime-Cilantro Remoulade
    (page 32), prepared

Thread several baby Yukon potatoes onto skewers so that they are just touching. In a small bowl, mix together the olive oil, vinegar, and bay leaf. Brush each skewer with the flavored olive oil and season with salt and pepper. Reserve the remaining flavored olive oil in the bowl.

Prepare a hot fire in your grill.

Place the potato skewers, tuna, and bowl of flavored oil on a doubled baking sheet. Carry everything out to the grill.

Grill the potato skewers for 10 to 15 minutes, turning often, or until they are blistered and soft. Baste with the flavored olive oil several times while grilling.

Grill the tuna steaks for 2½ to 3 minutes per side for medium-rare (3 to 4 minutes for medium). Baste with the flavored olive oil several times while grilling.

To serve, arrange the greens on each plate. Top with a grilled tuna steak, then remove the potatoes from the skewers and arrange along with the hard-boiled eggs, cherry tomatoes, and black olives. Pass the Lime-Cilantro Remoulade at the table.

LES SANDWICHES
SANDWICHES

The French were latecomers to the idea of a sandwich, made popular by the British Earl of Sandwich in the late eighteenth century.

Maybe that's because sandwiches are informal, "grab and go" casual eating. To the French, sandwiches are not a formal meal, but they are meant for a park bench, a sandy beach, or a wine bar. An open-face sandwich or tartine is considered a first course or appetizer.

Even the French idea of a barbecue is different than ours. Writes blogger Jamie Schler from her home in Nantes, in northwestern France: "Yes, the typical French barbecue is pretty much a replica of a sophisticated indoor dinner party, simply moved out onto the patio. Organized and orderly, just a handful of close friends, beautiful food and plenty of wine, the French concept of the outdoor barbecue or, for that matter, picnics, is just another meal, albeit al fresco."

Vive la différence!

Once you've tasted our Ooh-la-la Burger with Brie and Avocado (page 90) topped with a small round of grilled Brie and Avocado Relish, you'll be glad that bistro-style barbecue criss-crosses the proverbial pond so well. The classic Croque Monsieur on the Grill Griddle (page 93), Ham, Comté, and Apple sous la Brique (page 92), and Grilled Chicken Banh Mi (page 94) show that sandwiches with a French twist are very much at home on the North American patio.

TOASTED CROISSANTS
WITH GRILLED TOMATOES AND BACON

OOH-LA-LA CROISSANTS ON THE GRILL REALLY GET TOASTED. THE CHARRY, CRISPY grill marks only add to their allure—and their flavor. Choose tomatoes that are ripe but still firm. We suggest grilling only one side of the tomato slices so that they do not get mushy and fall apart on the grill.

SERVES 4

4 croissants, halved

Olive oil for brushing

3 medium-size tomatoes,
   cut into ⅜-inch-thick (0.75 cm) slices

Kosher salt and freshly ground black pepper

½ cup (113 g) Boursin cheese

4 teaspoons olive paste or tapenade

8 strips bacon, cooked crisp

8 to 12 fresh basil leaves

1 bunch fresh chives, snipped,
   about 2 ounces (60 g)

Prepare a medium-hot indirect fire in your grill.

Brush the cut side of the croissants with olive oil. Place the croissants cut-side down over the fire. Grill for 1 to 2 minutes, until browned. Move to the indirect side to keep warm.

Brush both sides of the tomatoes with olive oil and sprinkle with salt and pepper. Place the tomatoes directly over the fire. Grill on one side for 2 to 3 minutes, until tomato slices have good grill marks.

Spread one-fourth of the cheese on the bottom halves of croissants and one-fourth of the olive paste on the top halves. On bottom halves, layer with grilled tomato slices, bacon, basil, and snipped chives. Cover with croissant top halves and serve warm.

VARIATION:
Use other types of bread, such as ciabatta, challah, or sourdough, and cut them into ½-inch-thick (1 cm) slices.

TRUFFLED BRIOCHE
GRILLED CHEESE SANDWICHES

SUPERB GRILLED CHEESE SANDWICHES ARE IN A CLASS TO THEMSELVES. BRIOCHE bread—so buttery and delicious—is our favorite for this sandwich, but other breads like focaccia, ciabatta, and sourdough are very good substitutes.

SERVES 4

8 slices brioche, ¾ inch (1.5 cm) thick

4 tablespoons butter, melted

4 ounces (115 g) goat cheese, at room temperature

2 ounces (55 g) Neufchâtel cream cheese, at room temperature

1 bunch fresh chives, snipped, about 2 ounces (60 g)

2 ounces (56 g) fresh spinach leaves, coarsely chopped

2 ounces (55 g) Camembert cheese, at room temperature

1 to 2 tablespoons white truffle oil

Prepare a medium-hot fire in your grill.

Lightly brush one side of each slice of brioche with melted butter. Lay the slices of bread, butter-side down, on a baking sheet.

In a small bowl, combine the goat cheese and cream cheese and stir to blend. Spread the cheese mixture evenly on four of the brioche slices. Top with the chopped chives and spinach.

Thinly slice the Camembert and evenly distribute on top of the chives and spinach. Drizzle the truffle oil on each of the four naked slices of brioche and place those slices on top of the cheese.

Grill over the fire for about 3 to 4 minutes per side until the bread is browned with good grill marks and the cheese has melted. Slice in half and serve with Grilled Onion Soup (page 124).

GRILLED FRENCH GARDEN SANDWICHES

HERE'S A GOOD-FOR-YOU SANDWICH THAT EVERYONE WILL LOVE. YOU CAN USE store-bought roasted peppers in a jar or roast your own. To roast peppers, preheat the broiler or your grill to high. Broil or grill whole peppers until blackened, blistered, and tender. Place peppers in a brown paper bag and close the top. Set aside for about 5 minutes, until cool. Slice the peppers open to remove the core and seeds. Rub excess char off the skins. Use immediately or store in an airtight container in the refrigerator for up to 2 days. A batard is similar to a larger baguette, or you could use a loaf of Italian bread.

SERVES 4 TO 6

1 batard, halved lengthwise

Olive oil for brushing

½ cup (125 g) Four-Herb Pistou (page 27)

9 ounces (255 g) soft goat cheese

4 plum (Roma) tomatoes, sliced

Kosher salt and freshly ground black pepper

¾ cup (110 g) roasted red bell pepper strips (see note above)

½ cup (75 g) chopped drained canned or marinated artichoke hearts

¼ cup (40 g) pitted and sliced green olives

2 tablespoons chopped toasted walnuts (optional)

Prepare a medium-hot indirect fire in your grill.

Hollow out about one-third of the top half of the bread. Lightly brush the inside of both halves with olive oil. Spread pesto on the top half and goat cheese on the bottom half. On the bottom half, layer with tomato slices and season with salt and pepper. Layer with roasted peppers, artichoke hearts, green olives, and walnuts. Cover with the top half. Brush the sandwich all over with olive oil and wrap in foil.

Grill the sandwich over the fire for about 5 minutes per side, turning once, until heated through. Move to the indirect side, close the lid and grill for 10 minutes.

Cut sandwich into four or six slices and serve warm or at room temperature.

MINI LAMB BURGERS
WITH CILANTRO-MINT BUTTER

FOR A BOLD BURGER, YOU CAN'T BEAT THIS ONE, WITH ITS PUNGENT SPICES AND aromatic topping suggestive of the former French colonies in northern Africa—Morocco, Algeria, and Tunisia.

SERVES 4

Cilantro-Mint Butter

1/2 cup (113 g) unsalted butter,
   at room temperature

1 1/2 tablespoons finely chopped cilantro

1 1/2 tablespoons finely chopped mint

1 garlic clove, minced

1 pound (450 g) lean ground lamb

3 tablespoons fine dry breadcrumbs

2 tablespoons finely chopped green onion

1 teaspoon ground cumin

1 teaspoon ground coriander

1 teaspoon turmeric

1/2 teaspoon ground cinnamon

4 Kaiser rolls, hamburger buns, or pita breads

Lettuce, for garnish

Sliced tomato, cucumber, and onion, for garnish

For the Cilantro-Mint Butter, stir together the butter, cilantro, mint, and garlic in a small bowl. Set aside.

Prepare a medium-hot fire in your grill.

In a large bowl, using your hands, combine lamb, breadcrumbs, green onion, cumin, coriander, turmeric, and cinnamon. Form into four 1/2-inch-thick (1 cm) patties.

Grill the Kaiser rolls or hamburger buns cut-side down for 1 to 2 minutes until you get good grill marks. Spread with some of the butter and set aside.

Grill the burgers for 3 to 4 minutes per side, turning once, or until meat thermometer inserted in the center of a burger registers 160°F (75°C) for well done or to your liking.

Place each burger on a roll, top with additional butter, and garnish with lettuce, tomato, cucumber, and onion.

OOH-LA-LA BURGER WITH BRIE AND AVOCADO

THIS DECADENT VERSION OF A TRADITIONAL CHEESEBURGER HAS STYLE AND PANACHE, as well as great flavor. Grilling a whole baby Brie is a lot easier than you think. You just have to pay attention and take it off the grill the minute you see the cheese starting to ooze out of the rind. Then this soft gooey decadent cheese is divided and placed on top of the burger.

SERVES 4

Avocado Relish

1 large ripe avocado, pitted and diced

1 garlic clove, minced

¼ cup (5 g) finely minced fresh flat-leaf parsley

Olive oil for brushing

1 tablespoon freshly squeezed lime juice

Fine kosher or sea salt and
    freshly ground black pepper

1 pound (450 g) ground chuck,
    formed into four 1-inch-thick (2.5 cm) patties

4 seeded hamburger buns, Kaiser rolls,
    or ciabattini

Olive oil for brushing

1 large red onion, peeled and
    cut into ½-inch-thick (1 cm) slices

One 6-to-8-ounce wheel (170 to 227 g)
    baby Brie

Fine kosher or sea salt and
    freshly ground black pepper

1 large beefsteak tomato,
    cut into ½-inch (1-cm) slices

For the Avocado Relish, combine the avocado, garlic, parsley, olive oil, and lime juice in a bowl. Season with salt and pepper. Cover and set aside.

Prepare a hot fire in your grill.

Place the patties on a plate on a baking sheet. Brush the cut side of the buns with olive oil. Brush the red onion slices and the Brie with olive oil on both sides and season with salt and pepper. Place on the baking sheet to take out to the grill.

Grill the cut side of the buns for 1 to 2 minutes to lightly brown. Grill the onions, turning once, for 8 minutes. Grill the burgers, turning once, for 7 minutes for medium. Place the Brie in an aluminum pan and set beside the burgers and grill for 5 to 7 minutes, or until the cheese is *just beginning* to ooze out of the rind.

Place each burger on the bottom half of a bun and top with the grilled onions and a slice of tomato. Cut the Brie into four wedges and place a wedge on top of each burger. Place the top portion of the bun on each burger and serve immediately with the Avocado Relish on the side for diners to add to their burgers as they wish.

FRENCH-STYLE SANDWICHES ON THE GRILL

Enjoying a French-style sandwich on the grill is easy. Cut a baguette in half lengthwise, and tear out a little of the inner crumb so you'll have more room for fillings. Layer the baguette with fillings of your choice, then put the top back on. Brush the whole baguette with olive oil. Wrap the baguette with foil. Grill over medium heat with the grill lid closed, turning as necessary, until warmed through, about 20 minutes. Cut into crusty slices and serve with a napkin.

We've taken our inspiration for sandwich fillings from the various regions of France:

THE ALPES—Spread the inside of the baguette with unsalted butter, then layer on slices of the French Comté or Gruyére, plus finely chopped pickled plums, cornichons, or other preserved condiment to give a little sharpness.

THE AUVERGNE—Spread the inside of the baguette with unsalted butter, then layer on slices of Cantal, a medium-bodied cheese similar to Cheddar, and grilled leeks, shallots, or onion slices.

THE AVEYRON—Spread the inside of the baguette with unsalted butter, then spread with Roquefort and top with dollops of fig confiture or jam.

NORMANDY—Spread the inside of the baguette with unsalted butter, then layer on slices of Camembert with slices of a tart apple like Granny Smith.

PROVENCE—Brush the inside of the baguette with Pistou (page 27) or Aioli (page 29), then slather on fresh goat cheese. Top with sliced and pitted cured olives, roasted red peppers, and sliced fresh tomatoes.

HAM, COMTÉ, AND APPLE SOUS LA BRIQUE

SOUS LA BRIQUE MEANS "UNDER A BRICK." YOU PRESS THE SANDWICHES DOWN (LIKE paninis) as they grill. To do this, simply cover two bricks with foil, use a heavy cast-iron skillet as a weight, or simply press down hard on the panini with a heavy-duty grill spatula. Comté is from the Franche-Comté region in the Jura Mountains and is similar to Gruyère, which you can also use. Jambon de Bayonne is a French cured ham similar to Italian prosciutto and Spanish serrano ham. The key to the sandwich is thin flavorful ham. Thinly sliced cured Virginia ham or other artisan cured ham would be sublime.

SERVES 4

8 slices country-style French bread,
  ½ inch (1 cm) thick

Olive oil for brushing

8 ounces (250 g) Comté,
  rind removed and sliced

1 apple, cored and thinly sliced

8 thin slices ham

Prepare a medium-hot fire in the grill. Have a heavy cast-iron skillet, two foil-wrapped bricks, or a heavy-duty grill spatula by the grill.

Brush all sides of each slice of bread with olive oil. On the bottom portion of each sandwich, place the cheese, then the apple slices, and then the ham. Top with the remaining slice of bread. Place sandwiches on a baking sheet to take out to the grill.

Place two sandwiches on the grill at a time and weight or press down with the bricks. Grill for 3 to 4 minutes on each side, or until you have good grill marks and the cheese has melted. Then grill the other two sandwiches.

Slice each sandwich in half and serve hot.

CROQUE MONSIEUR ON THE GRILL GRIDDLE

ONE OF THE MOST POPULAR SANDWICHES AT A FRENCH CAFÉ IS THIS CRUNCHY ham and cheese sandwich. *Pain de mie* or brioche would be excellent French bread to use. The classic sandwich recipe uses crustless bread, but since the sandwich is supposed to be crunchy, keep the crust if you like. We use a grill griddle on the grill for this recipe because the cheese will ooze out of the sandwich and a griddle allows for easier clean up.

SERVES 4

Mornay Sauce

2 tablespoons unsalted butter

2 tablespoons flour

1½ cups (375 ml) whole milk, hot

¼ cup (30 g) Gruyère cheese, grated

¼ cup (30 g) Parmesan cheese, grated

¼ teaspoon hot sauce

Pinch of freshly ground nutmeg

8 slices bread ½ inch (1 cm) thick
   (like brioche, *pain de mie*, or sourdough)

4 tablespoons unsalted butter, melted

Dijon mustard

½ cup (60 g) ham, thinly sliced

½ cup (60 g) Gruyère
   or Emmental cheese, grated

Snipped chives, for garnish

Shavings of Gruyère, for garnish

For the Mornay Sauce, melt the butter over low heat in a small saucepan that can also be placed over the grill. Stir in the flour for about 2 minutes to make a paste (roux). Slowly add the hot milk, whisking constantly until the sauce is thickened. Remove from the heat and whisk in the cheeses, hot sauce, and nutmeg. Set aside.

Prepare a medium-hot fire in your grill and set a grill griddle on top of the fire.

Place the eight pieces of bread on a baking sheet and lightly brush one side with the melted butter and turn the bread butter-side down. Lightly brush mustard on four of the bread slices, and then evenly layer the ham and then the cheese. Top each with a buttered piece of bread. Take the sandwiches and Mornay sauce out to the grill. Set the saucepan over the heat and stir until hot but do not let boil. Place the sandwiches over the fire and grill for about 4 minutes until toasty and golden brown. Turn the sandwiches and grill for another 4 minutes until toasty. Serve the sandwiches with Mornay sauce spooned over the top with a sprinkling of snipped chives and shavings of Gruyère.

GRILLED CHICKEN BANH MI

TRUE FUSION FOOD FROM THE FRENCH OCCUPATION OF INDOCHINA, THE COMBINA-
tion of soft-crumbed French bread, grilled chicken, a sweet/sour crunchy relish
(known as Do chua), and aromatic cilantro make this an ideal hot-weather dish. This is also
a great way to use leftover grilled chicken.

SERVES 4 AS A MAIN COURSE

Carrot and Daikon Relish
1/2 cup (125 ml) rice wine vinegar

1 tablespoon granulated sugar

1/2 teaspoon kosher or sea salt

1 medium (2-ounce/60-g) carrot,
    peeled and julienned

1 small (1-ounce/30-g) daikon radish,
    peeled and julienned

4 boneless, skinless chicken breasts

Vegetable oil for brushing

Kosher salt and freshly ground black pepper

4 baguettes (10 inches/25 cm),
    sliced almost in half lengthwise

Unsalted butter, at room temperature,
    or mayonnaise for spreading

1 fresh jalapeño pepper, stemmed, seeded, and
    sliced lengthwise, very thinly, into strips

8 fresh cilantro sprigs

For the Carrot and Daikon Relish, stir the vinegar, sugar, and salt together in a medium
bowl. Then, stir in the vegetables. Set aside for 30 minutes.

Prepare a medium-hot fire in your grill.

Brush the chicken with vegetable oil and season with salt and pepper. Grill for 4 to
5 minutes on each side or until the chicken has good grill marks or until an instant-read
meat thermometer inserted in the thickest part of the chicken breast registers 160°F (75°C).
Let the chicken rest for 10 minutes.

Spread the cut sides of each baguette with butter. Cut each chicken breast into slices
and arrange on one half of the baguette. Top with 1/2 cup of the relish, a fourth of the jalapeño
slices, and two cilantro sprigs. Close the baguette and gently press down so that the juices
begin to permeate the bread. Serve immediately.

GRILLED TUNA PAN BAGNAT

PAN BAGNAT OR "BATHED BREAD" IS THE FRENCH MEDITERRANEAN'S VERSION OF a fast-food sandwich. Basically, they're crusty hard rolls, a round *boule,* or large baguettes slathered with vinaigrette, piled high with summer vegetables and black olives, maybe a little goat cheese or tuna, then pressed together so that all the juices permeate the sandwich. Grill ahead for this dish—enjoy grilled tuna earlier in the week and grill extra for this sandwich.

MAKES 4 SANDWICHES

Four 5-ounce (150-g) yellowfin tuna steaks

Olive oil for brushing

Kosher or sea salt and
 freshly ground black pepper

4 crusty rolls, ciabattini,
 or 1 baguette, sliced lengthwise

2 tablespoons red wine vinegar

1 teaspoon Dijon mustard

1 garlic clove, minced

1 teaspoon kosher or sea salt

1/2 teaspoon freshly ground black pepper

6 tablespoons olive oil

1 large 7-ounce (205-g) red onion,
 sliced into rings

1 large 9-ounce (280-g) cucumber, peeled,
 seeded, and cut into thin rounds

1 cup (180 g) chopped, pitted oil-cured olives

1 tomato, thinly sliced

2 handfuls of baby greens,
 such as arugula or spinach

Prepare a hot fire in your grill.

Brush the tuna with olive oil and season with salt and pepper.

Grill the tuna steaks for 2 1/2 to 3 minutes per side for medium-rare (3 to 4 minutes for medium).

Cut the rolls in half with a serrated knife. In a bowl, whisk the wine vinegar, Dijon mustard, garlic, salt, pepper, and olive oil together. Drench the cut sides of each roll with the vinaigrette. Arrange the tuna on the bottom cut side of each roll, and then layer on the vegetables, ending with the baby greens. Top with the other half of the roll and press down with the heel of your hand. Serve right away or wrap in waxed paper and serve at room temperature.

VARIATION:

Grilled Chicken Pan Bagnat is also *superbe.* Grill the chicken paillards according to the grilling directions in Grilled Chicken Banh Mi (page 94). To change it up a bit, omit the cucumber and substitute 1/4 cup (45 ml) capers for the olives. Assemble the sandwiches and enjoy.

LES PLATS D'ACCOMPAGNEMENT
SIDE DISHES

Main dishes or *les plats principaux* at a bistro are rounded out by generous helpings of hearty side dishes or *les plats d'accompagnement*. Some bistros serve these from a big bowl or gratin dish, while others plate them out for you.

The idea is to follow the seasons and use vegetables at their peak of freshness and flavor. In this chapter, we do the same.

In cold weather, the classic Potato Gratin (page 98) offers a silky-textured richness that pairs well with the slightly bitter flavor of foods that get a little char from the grill. Barbecued White Beans with Bacon and Pear (page 102) have a soupçon of enhanced flavor from the sweet pear and smoky bacon, vying with the traditional flageolet dish usually served with roast lamb.

In spring, Stir-Grill-Roasted Baby Beets with Lemon-Herb Butter (page 104), Grilled Onions with Thyme-Scented Cream (page 103), and Stir-Grilled Shallots with Tarragon Butter (page 106) offer more delicious options.

Then in summer and fall, Stir-Grilled Haricots Verts with Lemon Verbena Pistou (page 101), Grilled Ratatouille (page 109), and planked and roasted tomatoes come forward.

There is always a season for deliciousness.

POTATO GRATIN

NO BISTRO IS COMPLETE WITHOUT A GRATIN, A DISH OF POTATOES, LEEKS, fennel, or other vegetables that become soft and fragrant when baked. This one is adapted from our friend Ann Lund, author of the self-published *Dining in Style*. Soft rind cheeses melt lusciously into this dish, giving it a flavor so *c'est bien*. You infuse the half and half first with shallots and rosemary. Slice the potatoes with a mandoline or sharp knife by hand, or with the slicing blade on a food processor. This gratin sets up beautifully to enjoy with Grilled Lamb Chops, Paillard-Style (page 140), Spit-Roasted Chicken with Charred Tomatoes on the Vine (page 129), or Grill-Roasted Tenderloin with Bacon-Mushroom Sauce (page 169). Leftovers? *Mais oui!*

SERVES 12 TO 15

Butter for baking dish

3 cups (750 ml) half and half

3/4 cup (110 g) finely chopped shallot

2 teaspoons chopped fresh rosemary

2 teaspoons kosher or sea salt

3/4 teaspoon freshly ground black pepper

4 pounds (2 kg) russet potatoes,
    peeled and sliced 1/4 inch (.5 cm) thick

1 pound (455 g) soft rind cheese
    like Brie or Camembert

1 1/2 cups (135 g) Parmesan cheese, grated

Preheat the oven to 375°F (190°C). Butter a 13 x 9-inch (3 L) baking dish.

Pour the half and half into a large microwave-safe bowl and heat on high for 2 minutes. Or pour into a medium-size saucepan and warm over medium heat. Remove from the heat and stir in the shallot, rosemary, salt, and pepper. Cover and let infuse for 30 minutes.

Layer half the potato slices in the prepared baking dish, overlapping them to fit. Slice and layer half the soft rind cheese and sprinkle with half of the Parmesan cheese. Arrange the remaining potatoes on top of the cheese and pour the cream mixture over. Repeat the layering and sprinkling with the remaining cheese.

Cover with aluminum foil and bake for 1 hour. Remove the foil and bake until the top is golden and bubbling, about 45 minutes. Let cool for 10 minutes before cutting into squares.

THE CHEESES OF NORMANDY

The picturesque harbor town of Honfleur, on the Atlantic side of Normandy, has been an artist's retreat for over a century. The rolling countryside is dotted with pastures where Normande cattle, an ancient white breed with dark brown or black spots, graze. Honfleur boasts a thriving outdoor market where you can buy the tiny washed-rind, cow's milk cheeses of the region: Pont-L'Evêque, Livarot, Petit Pavé d'Auge, and Camembert. You'll also find the wonderful French butter from nearby Isigny. In France, these cheeses would be served with a simple green salad after the main course. In America, we would offer them as appetizers or include them in a rich and wonderful gratin.

STIR-GRILLED HARICOTS VERTS WITH LEMON VERBENA PISTOU

FRAGRANT LEMON VERBENA IS EXCELLENT PAIRED WITH THE FRESHEST BEANS you can get. You'll need to grow your own lemon verbena or lemon balm for this recipe. If you don't have either herb, then make and substitute the Four-Herb Pistou (page 27) instead. This recipe makes about 1 cup (250 ml) pistou. The extra is delicious served as an appetizer with crusty bread or dolloped on grilled chicken or fish. It can be stored in an airtight container in the refrigerator for up to 3 weeks or in the freezer for up to 3 months.

SERVES 4

Lemon Verbena Pistou

2 cloves garlic, chopped or minced

1 cup (225 ml) lightly packed fresh lemon verbena or lemon balm leaves

1/4 cup (20 g) freshly grated Parmesan cheese

1/4 cup (40 g) chopped walnuts

1/2 cup (125 ml) olive oil

Kosher salt and freshly ground black pepper

2 pounds (1 kg) haricots verts (slender green beans)

2 teaspoons olive oil

For the Lemon Verbena Pistou, purée the garlic, lemon verbena, Parmesan, and walnuts in a food processor. With the motor running, through the feed tube, gradually add olive oil in a steady stream. Season with salt and pepper and process the pistou until smooth. Set aside.

Prepare a hot fire in your grill. Set an oiled grill wok or basket over the fire.

In a bowl, toss beans with olive oil. Transfer to the wok or basket and stir-grill for 5 to 8 minutes, or until tender.

Toss beans with 1/4 cup (50 ml) of the pistou. Serve warm or let cool, refrigerate for up to 3 days, and serve cold.

BARBECUED WHITE BEANS WITH BACON AND PEAR

ANY TYPE OF PORK AND BEAN DISH TASTES SO MUCH SMOKIER AND RICHER WHEN it spends a little time on the grill. This one pairs well with grilled sausages or charcuterie, especially the Alsatian Knack (knackwurst), which is smoked pork in a white casing.

SERVES 8

Suggested wood: Apple, oak, or pear

4 large pears, peeled and diced

1 pound (450 g) dried white navy beans, soaked in water overnight, drained and rinsed

1 pound (450 g) smoked bacon, diced and cooked crisp

3 cups (700 ml) beer (preferably a pale lager)

1/4 cup (60 ml) light (fancy) molasses or pure maple syrup

1 teaspoon kosher or sea salt

1/2 teaspoon freshly ground black pepper

In a foil pan, combine pears, beans, bacon, beer, molasses, salt, and pepper. Set aside.

Prepare a hot indirect fire with a kiss of smoke (page 15) in your grill and add your desired type of wood. (Replenish the wood chips as necessary.)

When you see the first wisp of smoke, place the pan of beans on the indirect side of the grill. Close the lid and grill for 1 to 1¼ hours, adding a little water if necessary, until the beans have softened and thickened and have a good smoky aroma.

Serve this in a bowl, family-style.

VARIATION:

You can also slow smoke this dish. Simply prepare an indirect low fire for smoking in your grill or smoker; close the lid, and smoke for 2½ to 3 hours, or until the beans are tender.

SEEDS OF A FRENCH GARDEN

If you go to Paris and you're a gardener, a must-visit area is the Quai de la Mégisserie along the Seine near the Pont Neuf. There, you'll find a sometimes raucous display of plant and pet shops selling birds, fish, and other animals. You'll also find a famous French seed house—Vilmorin—founded in 1743. At Vilmorin, you can buy a packet of seeds to grow Basilic Pistou (the preferred basil variety for the Provençal pistou), eleven different varieties of the salad green known as *mâche*, many kinds of tiny green *filet* beans for haricots verts, and even the Cinderella pumpkin Rouge Vif d'Etampes. In North America, you can also find French seeds through Renee Shepherd at *reneesgarden.com* or *cooksgarden.com*, now part of W. Atlee Burpee & Co.

GRILLED ONIONS
WITH THYME-SCENTED CREAM

THESE GRILLED WHOLE ONIONS, TOPPED WITH THYME-SCENTED CREAM, ARE A FAB-ulous accompaniment to grilled steaks or pork chops. If you want to grill everything at the same time, you'll need a hot fire for the meat but a cooler spot for the onions—perhaps along the perimeter of the grill or on an elevated rack. Or you can grill these alone over a medium fire.

SERVES 4

6 to 8 small yellow or white onions, peeled (about 1 pound/450 g)

Olive oil for brushing

2 garlic cloves, minced

1 cup (250 ml) heavy whipping cream

1 teaspoon fresh thyme leaves (or ½ teaspoon dried)

½ teaspoon fine kosher or sea salt

½ teaspoon freshly ground black pepper

Prepare a medium fire in your grill.

Using a grapefruit spoon or paring knife, cut out a 1-inch (2.5-cm) diameter core from the top of each onion. Brush the bottoms with olive oil and place in an aluminum pan.

In a bowl, whisk together garlic, cream, thyme, salt, and pepper. Spoon about 1 table-spoon into each onion, letting some drizzle down the sides. Reserve the remaining cream mixture.

Place the pan of onions on the grill. Close the lid and grill for 10 to 15 minutes. Baste with some of the cream mixture, close the lid and grill for 10 to 15 minutes more or until onions are browned and softened. Serve with the remaining cream spooned on top.

STIR-GRILL-ROASTED BABY BEETS WITH LEMON-HERB BUTTER

FRESH BEETS ARE SWEET AND DELICIOUS. WHETHER YOU USE THE DARK RUBY-colored, white, orange, or striped beets, the contrast in color with the green onions is very striking. To get the best flavor without the beets drying out during grilling, we par-cook the beets first, then stir-grill them. Slices of country bread on the side are nice for sopping up the extra butter.

SERVES 4

20 baby beets, trimmed (about 1 pound/450 g)

Kosher or sea salt and
    freshly ground black pepper

8 green onions, cut into 3-inch (6-cm) pieces

Lemon-Herb Butter

1/2 cup (113 g) unsalted butter, softened

2 garlic cloves, minced

2 tablespoons chopped fresh herbs, such as dill,
    oregano, thyme, or parsley

2 teaspoons freshly squeezed lemon juice

In a pot of boiling water, boil the beets for 10 to 15 minutes, or until tender enough to pierce with a fork. Drain, rinse in cold water, and pat dry. Set aside.

For the Lemon-Herb Butter, melt the butter over medium-high heat in a small sauce-pan. Add the garlic and sauté for 1 minute, or until fragrant. Remove from the heat and stir in the herbs and lemon juice. Set aside.

Prepare a hot fire in your grill.

Place the beets in an oiled grill wok or basket and set on top of a baking sheet. Drizzle beets with some of the butter, tossing to coat. Season with salt and pepper.

Place the wok on the grill. Stir-grill for about 8 minutes, basting occasionally with Lemon-Herb Butter and tossing with wooden paddles or grill spatulas, until the beets are charred. Add green onions and stir-grill for 4 minutes, basting with Lemon-Herb Butter, until the onions are charred. Transfer to a platter and serve with the remaining butter on the side.

STIR-GRILLED SHALLOTS WITH TARRAGON BUTTER

MAKE THE FULL RECIPE EVEN IF YOU ARE DINING WITH FEWER PEOPLE. THIS DISH is excellent alongside Lavender-Smoked Rack of Lamb (page 145) and Basque-Style Pork Paillards with Red Peppers (page 174). Leftover grilled shallots can be chopped and served over any meat dish or added to salads, soups, sandwiches, dips, and tartines.

SERVES 4

10 to 12 shallots (about 1 pound/450 g)
Kosher or sea salt and
   freshly ground black pepper

Tarragon Butter

1 garlic clove, minced
1/2 cup (113 g) unsalted butter, softened
1 tablespoon chopped fresh tarragon
1 teaspoon tarragon vinegar
1 loaf crusty French bread

Prepare a hot fire in your grill.

Pull shallot sections apart if necessary, but do not peel. Place in an oiled grill wok or basket and season to taste with salt and pepper. Set aside.

For the Tarragon Butter, combine garlic, butter, tarragon, and vinegar in a small bowl. Set aside.

Place the grill wok or basket with the shallot sections on the grill. Stir-grill for about 15 minutes, or until skins are charred and some of the flesh is exposed and golden, with a bit of caramel ooze. Let cool for 3 to 4 minutes, and then slip off the skins.

Meanwhile, wrap the loaf of bread in foil and heat on the grill for about 2 minutes per side.

Place shallots in a shallow dish, add the butter, and toss to coat. Slice or tear the hot bread and serve with the bowl of buttery shallots.

PLANKED GOAT CHEESE–TOPPED BEEFSTEAK TOMATOES

FRENCH VILLAGES HAD THE VILLAGE BAKER, WHO WOULD FIRE UP THE WOOD-burning oven and allow the villagers to bake their gratins and stuffed vegetables after the bread baking was finished. We have the covered grill and an aromatic wood plank to do a similar job. Planking vegetables is so easy, because they don't really need to cook through. Letting them sit on the warmed plank allows them to pick up a bit of its aromatic wood flavor along with the flavor of the grill.

SERVES 6 TO 8

1 to 2 oak, cedar, or maple planks,
 soaked in water for at least 1 hour

2 to 3 large tomatoes (such as beefsteak), sliced
 about ¾ inch (1.5 cm) thick

Kosher or sea salt and
 freshly ground black pepper

Extra-virgin olive oil

4 ounces (113 g) goat cheese

¼ cup (60 ml) chopped fresh herbs
 (such as chives, oregano, parsley, or basil)

Balsamic vinegar

Prepare a medium-hot indirect fire in your grill.

Arrange tomato slices on plank(s). Season the tomatoes lightly with salt and pepper and drizzle with olive oil. Crumble goat cheese over each tomato slice.

Place plank(s) on the indirect side of the grill. Close the lid and plank for about 15 to 20 minutes, or until tomatoes are warmed through and cheese is soft. Serve on the plank(s) with a sprinkle of fresh herbs and a drizzle of balsamic vinegar.

VARIATIONS:

Prepare a variety of colorful heirloom tomatoes. Slice larger tomatoes, quarter smaller ones, and halve cherry tomatoes. Arrange on the plank(s) and follow the rest of the steps above.

Use crumbled blue cheese or French feta or shredded Cheddar cheese in place of the goat cheese.

PROVENÇAL GRILL-ROASTED TOMATOES

THESE ROBUSTLY FLAVORED STUFFED TOMATOES GIVE GRILLED FISH, SHELLFISH, chicken, lamb, or beef a Mediterranean flair. Start the tomatoes on the indirect side, and then grill the meat on the direct side.

SERVES 6

12 ripe but firm tomatoes, about 3 pounds (1.5 kg)

¼ cup (50 ml) olive oil

⅓ cup (75 ml) minced onion

2 tablespoons anchovy paste

2 cups (150 g) lightly toasted fresh breadcrumbs

1 tablespoon finely chopped garlic

1 tablespoon finely chopped fresh flat-leaf parsley

2 tablespoons capers

Core the tomatoes. With the tip of a spoon, remove as many of the seeds as you can while leaving the pulp intact. Turn the tomatoes upside down to drain on paper towels.

In a skillet, heat the olive oil over medium heat and sauté the chopped onion until golden, about 5 minutes. Add the anchovy paste and stir until dissolved. Remove from the heat and stir in the breadcrumbs, garlic, parsley, and capers.

Place the tomatoes right-side up in foil pan and stuff with the breadcrumb mixture. Set aside.

Prepare a hot indirect fire in your grill.

Place the pan on the indirect side of the grill. Close the lid and grill for 20 to 30 minutes, or until tomatoes are softened and the tops are browned. Serve hot or at room temperature.

GRILLED RATATOUILLE

DIFFERENT FROM THE CLASSIC RATATOUILLE THAT IS MORE LIKE A STEW, THIS grilled version has a bit of texture and crunch to it and is very colorful. For a main dish, this may be served tossed with pasta. This recipe includes enough vegetables for 1 pound (500 g) dried pasta, cooked. If you omit the anchovy paste, it's also a wonderful vegan dish that you can serve with baguettes that have been sliced, their cut sides brushed with olive oil, and grilled.

SERVES 8

2 Japanese eggplants, about 12 ounces (350 g), stemmed and cut into 1-inch (2.5-cm) slices

2 large red onions, cut into 1-inch (2.5-cm) slices

2 yellow bell peppers, cored, seeded, and quartered

1 zucchini, about 6 ounces (175 g), halved lengthwise

3 firm ripe tomatoes, cut in half, about 18 ounces (550 g)

Olive oil for brushing

2 tablespoons anchovy paste

3 garlic cloves, finely chopped

1 cup (250 ml) extra-virgin olive oil

Kosher or sea salt and freshly ground black pepper

2 tablespoons finely sliced fresh basil, for garnish

1 tablespoon capers, for garnish

Prepare a hot fire in your grill.

Set the prepared vegetables on a baking sheet and brush them lightly with olive oil.

Combine the anchovy paste and garlic and whisk in the olive oil. Set aside.

Place the eggplant and onions on the grill and grill for about 4 or 5 minutes per side until browned and supple. Remove from the grill and set back on the sheet. Place the peppers skin-side down on the grill and the zucchini and tomatoes cut-side down on the grill and grill until browned, about 4 or 5 minutes. Remove from the grill and set back on the sheet.

Chop all the grilled vegetables and place in a large bowl. Toss with the anchovy paste mixture. Mix well and season with salt and pepper to taste. Garnish with basil and capers. The dish may be served immediately or holds well for several hours. Serve at room temperature.

LEGUMES
VEGETABLE MAIN COURSES

When cooked on the grill, vegetables can taste so good that it's no sacrifice for even a meat-lover to enjoy them as a main course.

The recipes in this chapter make delicious vegetarian options for the *plat principal* but are also delicious as side dishes or first courses. There are vegetables to grill all year long, and, in this chapter, you'll find recipes to grill them perfectly.

When you cut a vegetable lengthwise into thin, long slices mimicking the more common chicken or pork paillards, you get a quickly grilled option that works for cauliflower, zucchini, yellow summer squash, and eggplant. Pair the vegetable paillards with a colorful, vegetable-based sauce, and they're even more delicious.

Grill-roasting—grilling foods with an indirect fire and the grill lid closed—works well for root vegetables, so we serve them up here in a Smoked Garlic Aioli Platter of Roasted Root Vegetables (page 120). Once you try Grill-Roasted Pumpkin with Dry-Cured Olives and Garlic (page 114), it could become a fixture on your fall grilling menu.

GRILLED CAULIFLOWER PAILLARDS WITH ORANGE–OLIVE PISTOU

IN *THE GARDENER AND THE GRILL, WE GRILLED CAULIFLOWER SLICES THEN TOPPED* them with a tomatillo salsa, but when we saw Jason Neroni's vegan dish served at Superba Snack Bar in Los Angeles, we said "ooh-la-la!" and adapted it here. One large cauliflower will yield about six (1-inch/2.5-cm) paillards, with two of the slices being the end pieces. Only cut part of the core, because if you remove too much, the paillard will fall apart.

SERVES 2 TO 3

Orange-Olive Pistou

¼ cup (50 ml) extra-virgin olive oil

Juice of 1 lemon

2 oranges (14 ounces/435 g), peeled, segmented, and coarsely chopped

½ cup (90 g) green olives (such as Manzanilla or Picholine), pitted and coarsely chopped

¼ cup (40 g) golden raisins

2 garlic cloves, finely chopped

2 tablespoons coarsely chopped flat-leaf parsley

Kosher or sea salt and freshly ground black pepper

1 large head (2½ pounds/1.25 kg) cauliflower, part of core and green leaves removed

Olive oil for brushing

Kosher or sea salt

Prepare an indirect medium-hot fire in your grill.

For the Orange-Olive Pistou, stir the olive oil, lemon juice, orange segments, olives, raisins, garlic, and parsley together in a bowl. Season with salt and pepper and set aside.

Cut the cauliflower from top to bottom into 1-inch-thick (2.5 cm) slices and place on a baking sheet. Brush the cauliflower with olive oil and salt to taste. Place the cauliflower slices over the hot fire and grill for 2 minutes per side to get good grill marks, and then move to the indirect or no-heat side of the grill. Close the lid and grill-roast for another 10 minutes, until the cauliflower slices still hold together but are tender when pierced with a fork.

To serve, shingle or overlap the cauliflower slices on a platter and spoon the Orange-Olive Pistou down the center.

GRILL-ROASTED PUMPKIN
WITH DRY-CURED OLIVES AND GARLIC

IN FRENCH MARKETS IN AUTUMN, YOU WILL SEE HUGE *POTIRONS*, SUCH AS THE ROUGE Vif d'Etampes, known as the Cinderella pumpkin because it looks like the carriage brought to life by her fairy godmother. There, they sell slices from a whole pumpkin that you can bring to life by roasting at home. Here, you can simply buy a small sugar or pie pumpkin, cut it into slices, and then grill-roast this simple yet satisfying dish that will completely change how you think about pumpkin.

SERVES 6

¼ cup (50 ml) extra-virgin olive oil

3 large garlic cloves, sliced

1 small pumpkin (about 1½ pounds/750 g) or 1 medium-size butternut or Hubbard squash, stemmed, seeded, and cut into 2-inch (5-cm) wedges (at the widest part)

20 black, dry-cured olives, pitted and halved

1 teaspoon chopped fresh thyme, or ½ teaspoon dried thyme

Kosher or sea salt and freshly ground black pepper

Prepare a medium-hot fire in your grill.

In a saucepan over medium heat, warm the oil and garlic together until the garlic is fragrant, about 4 minutes.

Arrange the pumpkin slices, olives, and thyme in disposable aluminum pans. Drizzle with the olive oil mixture, and then season with salt and pepper.

Place on the grill, close the lid, and grill for 20 minutes. Open the lid and turn the pumpkin slices over. Close the lid and grill for 15 to 20 minutes more or until the pumpkin is fork-tender. Transfer the pumpkin wedges to a platter and drizzle with the juices from the pan. Sprinkle the olives over the pumpkin and serve warm.

PROVENÇAL-STYLE STUFFED SMOKED VEGETABLES

In the south of France, *legumes farcis à la provençale*, such as tomatoes, peppers, and zucchini, are so beloved that small varieties perfect for stuffing remain popular. Meat and breadcrumb stuffings are traditional, but we love the simplicity and deliciousness of goat cheese with a drizzle of olive oil and that kiss of smoke. Use this recipe as a blueprint for an easy meal with big flavor and lovely color.

Serves 6

Suggested wood: Almond, apple, cherry, oak, or pecan

6 medium Striped Cavern or Roma tomatoes, Ronde de Nice
or small round zucchini, or small bell peppers

6 ounces (175 g) goat cheese, or more

4 ounces (125 g) fresh greens

Fresh basil or mint

Olive oil and balsamic vinegar (fig flavored if possible) for drizzling

With a serrated knife, core the tomatoes, zucchini, or bell peppers and scrape out some of the interior seeds. Stuff each vegetable with 1 ounce (30 g) of soft goat cheese. Arrange the vegetables upright in a disposable aluminum pan and drizzle with olive oil. If necessary, lightly trim the bottom of a vegetable so it sits evenly in the pan.

Prepare an indirect fire with a kiss of smoke (page 15) in your grill and add your desired type of wood. When you see the first wisp of smoke, place the pan of stuffed vegetables on the indirect or no-heat side and close the lid. Smoke the vegetables for 45 minutes or until they are burnished on top and have a good, smoky aroma. Arrange the greens on a platter and place the stuffed vegetables on the greens. Garnish with sprigs of fresh herbs and then drizzle with more olive oil and a little balsamic vinegar.

VEGETABLE PAILLARDS WITH FRENCH FETA SPREAD

AS WITH THE GRILLED CAULIFLOWER PAILLARDS WITH ORANGE-OLIVE PISTOU (page 113), you can also turn other vegetables into paillards, or thin slices that cook quickly. As an appetizer with grilled bread, a side dish, or a main dish, this recipe has rock-star quality. The French feta cheese, made from sheep's milk, is creamy, rich, and tangy. Choose squash and eggplants that will be about the same length and width when sliced. If you like, add a dipping sauce of Lemon-Tarragon Vinaigrette (page 26) or simply extra-virgin olive oil. Be sure to brush slices of good crusty bread with olive oil and grill along with the paillards.

SERVES 4

French Feta Spread

1 cup (8 ounces/227 g) crumbled French feta cheese (such as the Valbreso brand)

1 tablespoon extra-virgin olive oil

1 garlic clove, minced

1/2 cup (90 g) finely chopped Kalamata or Niçoise olives

2 tablespoons finely chopped chives or green onions

1 teaspoon grated lemon zest

One Japanese eggplant, about 6 ounces (175 g), ends trimmed and cut lengthwise into 1/2-inch-thick (1 cm) strips

One zucchini, about 6 ounces (175 g), ends trimmed and cut lengthwise into 1/2-inch-thick (1 cm) strips

One yellow summer squash, about 6 ounces (175 g), ends trimmed and cut lengthwise into 1/2-inch-thick (1 cm) strips

Olive oil for brushing

Kosher or sea salt and freshly ground black pepper

6 sprigs of flat-leaf parsley, for garnish

Prepare a hot fire in your grill.

For the French Feta Spread, combine the cheese, olive oil, garlic, olives, chives, and lemon zest in a bowl and stir until well blended. Set aside.

Brush the eggplant, zucchini, and yellow summer squash slices with olive oil and season with salt and pepper. Place on a baking sheet to take out to the grill.

Grill the eggplant slices for 4 to 5 minutes on each side, and the squash for 2 or 3 minutes on one side only, or until you have good grill marks and the vegetable slices are soft and charred. Transfer vegetables to the sheet and bring back inside.

While the slices are still warm from the grill, slather each eggplant slice with some of the feta spread, top with a yellow squash slice, slather more spread, then top with a zucchini slice to create a stack. If you like, arrange the paillard stacks on a platter or cut into 1-inch (2.5-cm) squares. Serve warm or at room temperature, garnished with the parsley.

POTAGER ON A PLATTER RUSTIQUE

A *JARDIN POTAGER* IS A KITCHEN GARDEN. OFTEN, IT'S CLOSE TO THE KITCHEN door for snipping fresh herbs or harvesting tomatoes or leeks from nearby pots or a patch of ground. Since this is a platter of assorted vegetables, think about their sizes and seasonality as you pick or purchase them. Add herbs to the platter for an eye-appealing pop of green garnish. With a pot of parsley nearby, Persillade Drizzle is quick to fix. It's a fragrant mixture of parsley and fresh garlic chopped together and used as a flavorful garnish for soups, stews, chicken casseroles, shellfish, fish, fresh sliced tomatoes, and other vegetables. We add lemon juice and olive oil to make it a drizzle. The vegetables we have listed in this recipe may all be used for the platter or you may pick and choose what is available. The vegetables require a minimum of halving or slicing, and we don't even core the peppers, thus the *rustique* in the title.

SERVES 8

Persillade Drizzle

3 cups (75 g) loosely packed fresh parsley leaves

4 garlic cloves, roughly chopped

2 tablespoons lemon juice

1 cup (250 ml) extra-virgin olive oil

4 pounds (2 kg) mixed seasonal garden vegetables (such as summer squash, romaine, fennel, bok choy, leeks, endive, bell peppers, tomatoes, eggplant, and onions)

Olive oil for brushing

Kosher or sea salt and freshly ground black pepper

For the Persillade Drizzle, place the parsley and garlic in a food processor and process until finely minced. Then slowly add the lemon juice and olive oil. Set aside.

Prepare a hot fire in your grill.

Slice the squash, romaine, fennel, bok choy, leeks, endive, and peppers in half lengthwise. Cut tomatoes, eggplant, and onions into 1-inch-thick (2.5 cm) slices. Brush the cut side of the halved vegetables with olive oil, except brush the peppers on their skin side. Brush the other sliced vegetables with oil on both sides. Season with salt and pepper.

Place the squash, romaine, fennel, bok choy, leeks, and endive cut-side down on the grill. Place the peppers skin-side down. Grill for about 4 or 5 minutes, until the cut sides and pepper skins have good grill marks.

Grill the tomatoes, eggplant, and onions for 3 to 4 minutes on one side, set the tomatoes aside, and turn the eggplant and onions on the other side and grill until charry on both sides.

Arrange the grilled vegetables on a large platter and spoon the Persillade Drizzle over all. Serve hot or at room temperature.

GRILLED EGGPLANT
WITH GRUYÈRE AND SUN-DRIED TOMATOES

THIS DISH IS SIMILAR TO EGGPLANT PARMESAN, BUT WITH A FRENCH TWIST. FOR the best results, always oil the eggplant right before you grill it, since eggplant absorbs the oil so quickly. Sun-dried tomatoes are available in sealable bags or in jars with olive oil. We prefer the bagged variety, as they are supple and very flavorful.

SERVES 4 TO 6

2 small eggplants (about 2 pounds/1 kg)

Kosher or sea salt

1 garlic clove, finely minced

½ cup (125 ml) extra-virgin olive oil

2 tablespoons dried oregano, crumbled

¼ cup (30 g) chopped sun-dried tomatoes

½ cup (60 g) shredded Gruyère cheese

Fresh herbs, for garnish

Slice the ends off the eggplants, but do not peel. Cut lengthwise into ½-inch-thick (1 cm) slices and lightly salt. Place in a colander and let drain for at least 30 minutes to remove excess water. Pat dry.

Meanwhile, prepare a medium-hot fire in your grill.

In a bowl, combine the garlic, olive oil, and oregano. Brush on both sides of the eggplant slices when you are ready to grill.

Grill the eggplant for about 10 minutes, turning once, until tender with good grill marks.

Arrange the slices attractively on a platter and sprinkle with sun-dried tomatoes and shredded cheese while the eggplant is hot. Garnish with fresh herbs.

SMOKED GARLIC AIOLI PLATTER
OF ROASTED ROOT VEGETABLES

SOMETIMES THE SIMPLEST THINGS PACK THE MOST FLAVOR. TENDER ROOT VEGE-tables grilled with a kiss of smoke taste even more delectable when served with Smoked Garlic Aioli (page 29). Par-cooking the vegetables first helps them smoke-roast more quickly. If you like, place individual garlic cloves in the aluminum pans to smoke-roast with the vegetables, and then make the Smoked Garlic Aioli.

SERVES 6 TO 8

Suggested wood: A mix of oak and apple

4 pounds (2 kg) mixed root vegetables
(such as sweet potatoes, white potatoes,
carrots, turnips, onions)

Olive oil for brushing

Kosher or sea salt and
freshly ground black pepper

1 recipe Smoked Garlic Aioli (page 29)

Prepare a medium-hot indirect fire with a kiss of smoke in your grill (page 15).

Scrub the potatoes, leaving the skin on, and cut into wedges. Rinse and peel the carrots, turnips, and onions. Leave the carrots whole and cut the turnips and onions into wedges. Microwave the vegetables, in batches, for 3 to 4 minutes on high or until partially cooked.

Brush the vegetables with olive oil. Place the vegetables in disposable aluminum pans.

When you see the first wisp of smoke, place the vegetables on the indirect side of the grill. Close the lid and smoke for about 1 hour, or until the vegetables are fork-tender.

Arrange the vegetables on a platter, season with salt and pepper, and drizzle lightly with olive oil. Serve with Smoked Garlic Aioli on the side.

VARIATION:

Winter squash (such as acorn or butternut), while not a root vegetable, would be a nice addition to this medley. Peel and cut into 1-inch-thick (2.5 cm) strips and prepare as above.

TOASTED BARLEY PILAF
WITH GRILLED GARDEN VEGETABLES

WHOLE GRAINS LIKE BARLEY, PREPARED AS ENTRÉES OR ACCOMPANIMENTS, ARE the kind of dishes that people say, "I haven't had barley in a long time and I love it. Why don't we think to prepare it more often?" Well, there is no reason to forsake barley. It is a wonderful staple to have in your pantry. In this preparation, it is toasted first in a dry skillet to give it a nuttier flavor. Then you add liquid, and the barley simmers like a rice pilaf, but it never gets as soft and gummy as rice sometimes does. When you add the grill-roasted chopped vegetables, they look like precious gems. A finish of lemon zest brightens and keeps everything fresh, perfect for *le pique-nique*.

SERVES 6 TO 8

1½ cups (235 g) pearl barley

4 cups (1 L) chicken broth

2 bay leaves

1 teaspoon kosher or sea salt

4 carrots, about 12 ounces (335 g), peeled and chopped

1 yellow onion, about 6 ounces (175 g), peeled and chopped

1 red bell pepper, about 7 ounces (185 g), cored and chopped

1 tablespoon olive oil

Kosher or sea salt and freshly ground black pepper

2 green onions, chopped

Zest of 1 lemon

To toast the barley, place it in a dry skillet over medium-high heat for 8 to 10 minutes, stirring occasionally until most of the barley is a medium-golden brown. Transfer barley to a Dutch oven, add 4 cups of chicken broth, and bring to a boil. Add the bay leaves and salt. Cover and cook at a simmer for about 30 minutes until barley is tender. Add ½ cup (125 ml) or more of water if the broth is absorbed before the barley is done. Remove the bay leaves and set aside.

Prepare a hot indirect fire in your grill.

Place the chopped carrots, onion, and pepper in an aluminum pan. Drizzle with the olive oil and season with salt and pepper.

Place the pan of vegetables on the indirect side of the grill. Close the lid and grill-roast for about 15 minutes or until the vegetables are tender.

Add the vegetables, green onions, and lemon zest to the barley and stir to blend.

Serve warm, at room temperature, or chill in the refrigerator and serve cold.

VARIATIONS:

Chicken Barley Soup with Grilled Vegetables is so simple to make with any leftovers (*les restes*) of this recipe. Just add the amount of chopped grilled chicken and chicken stock to the barley mixture that you desire. The chopped grill-roasted vegetables are perfect in any vegetable soup, gazpacho, or even a cheesy broccoli soup.

GRILLING SAVOIR FAIRE

It's always a good idea to grill more than you need for one meal. Grilled leftovers keep their color and flavor better than other cooked foods. You already know what to do with leftover grilled chicken, steak, pork, fish, or shellfish. But what about other foods?

Here are a few ideas.

- Grilling bread? Grill more to use for appetizers or spreads a few days later or cube the toasty bread to use for croutons in salads or soups. Store the grilled bread in plastic storage bags at room temperature.

- Preparing the Grilled Ratatouille (page 109)? Grill more and use it in the wonderful Grilled Red Pepper and Tomato Soup with Goat Cheese Croutons (page 125). Store it in the refrigerator.

- Making the Stir-Grilled Shallots with Tarragon Butter (page 106)? Grill extra shallots to chop and add to Grilled Onion Soup with Flame-Licked Croutons (page 124). Store it in the refrigerator.

- Finishing your meal with grilled fruit? Add any leftovers to your breakfast yogurt, and then drizzle lavender or wildflower honey over it all. Store it in the refrigerator.

GRILLED ONION SOUP
WITH FLAME-LICKED CROUTONS

FRENCH ONION SOUP IS A CULT CLASSIC THAT IS RUMORED TO HAVE ORIGINATED AT the old Les Halles Market in Paris. In the traditional recipe, you caramelize onions on the stovetop, and then add beef broth to make soup. But guess what? You can also caramelize onions on the grill, where they take on an even more pronounced flavor. If you want to keep this recipe vegetarian, use a good quality vegetable broth in place of chicken or beef.

SERVES 6

2 large (2 pounds/1 kg) white onions

12 slices baguette

Olive oil for brushing

12 ounces (375 g) freshly grated Gruyère
  or Comté cheese

2 tablespoons butter

½ teaspoon salt

1 cup (500 ml) dry white wine

¼ cup (50 ml) dry sherry

8 cups (2 L) broth—chicken, beef,
  or a combination of both

Prepare an indirect hot fire in your grill.

Slice the onions ¾ inch (1.5 cm) thick and thread each slice onto a wooden skewer that has been soaked in water for 30 minutes. Brush the onion "lollipops" and the slices of bread with olive oil. Set on a baking sheet.

Grill the onions for about 5 to 7 minutes per side until charred and soft. Grill the bread for about 1 to 2 minutes per side until toasted with good grill marks. Top the bread with 2 tablespoons of the cheese and set on the indirect side of the grill for a couple of minutes or until the cheese melts. Set aside. When the onions are cool, remove them from the skewers and chop. Set aside.

Melt the butter in a stockpot and add the chopped grilled onions and salt. Sauté for a couple of minutes over low heat. Add the wine and sherry and simmer for 15 minutes. Add the broth and bring to a boil, then simmer for 30 minutes.

Spoon the soup into six bowls and top with two cheesy croutons and sprinkle the remaining grated cheese among the bowls. Serve at once.

GRILLED RED PEPPER AND TOMATO SOUP WITH GOAT CHEESE CROUTONS

HOT OFF THE GRILL AND WHIRLED IN A BLENDER OR FOOD PROCESSOR, THIS EASY soup makes a traditional tomato soup and grilled cheese sandwich sound so, well, *insipide*. If you want to keep this vegetarian, use good-quality vegetable broth or stock in place of chicken.

SERVES 4

4 cups (1 L) good-quality chicken
   or vegetable broth

2 large red bell peppers (about 6 ounces/180 g)

8 large beefsteak tomatoes
   (about 4 pounds/2 kg)

2 large garlic cloves, minced

1/4 cup (50 ml) olive oil

Kosher or sea salt and
   freshly ground black pepper

Goat Cheese Croutons

8 slices baguette

Olive oil for brushing

8 ounces (227 g) fresh goat cheese

1/4 cup (50 ml) chopped fresh basil

Prepare a hot fire in your grill.

Bring the chicken or vegetable broth to a simmer in a saucepan.

Cut each bell pepper in half lengthwise. Remove the stems and seeds. Core the tomatoes. In a small bowl, combine the garlic and olive oil and brush the vegetables. Reserve the remaining garlic olive oil.

Grill the peppers for about 4 to 5 minutes per side until charred and soft. Grill the tomatoes for 2 to 3 minutes per side, turning once, or until they have good grill marks and have slightly softened.

For the Goat Cheese Croutons, brush the bread with some of the reserved garlic olive oil and grill for about 2 minutes per side until toasted with good grill marks. Top the bread with 1 ounce (30 g) of the cheese and sprinkle with fresh basil.

Quickly skin and deseed the grilled tomatoes. Place the grilled peppers, skinned and deseeded tomatoes, and any remaining reserved garlic olive oil in a blender or food processor and purée. Add the simmering stock and carefully blend again. Season with salt and pepper. Spoon into bowls and serve topped with Goat Cheese Croutons.

VOLAILLE
POULTRY

The last time we were in France with a group of friends, we tried to find a *poulet de Bresse*, or the finest poultry available, so we could roast it and see if it lived up to the hype. We did find one—at a *boucherie* in Monte Carlo—but the day was hot and we didn't have a way to keep it cool enough to take back to the cottage we were renting. Ah, missed opportunities!

A *poulet de Bresse* still has some of the feathers attached, and its feet have a numbered metal band that traces the chicken back to the exact Rhône-Alpes farm and brood from which it hatched. Ultimate accountability!

In America, we recommend using a free-range chicken or turkey from a local farm to get the best and freshest flavor.

Then, there are so many grilling techniques to use. For the whole bird, Spit-Roasted Chicken with Charred Tomatoes on the Vine (page 129) echoes the popular French rotisserie bistros. You can also de-backbone and then flatten a chicken for Spatchcocked Chicken with Rosemary Sprigs (page 136). You can stuff a chicken breast with any number of mixtures after you try Brie and Tapenade–Stuffed Chicken Breast (page 135). Slather a chicken breast with a flavorful mixture and cook it *a la plancha* in Planked Chicken Breasts with Artichoke Slather (page 131). Or simply slice and pound thin a boneless, skinless chicken breast to make Bistro Chicken Paillards (page 128), really, really fast food on your grill.

BISTRO CHICKEN PAILLARDS

PAILLARD IS A FRENCH TERM MEANING A VERY THIN BONELESS AND SKINLESS PIECE of chicken, veal, lamb, pork, or even vegetable. Pounded to just 1/2 inch (1 cm) of thickness, chicken paillards grill in just 5 minutes over a hot fire. That's really fast food! Serve this with sliced tomatoes and crusty French bread or Goat Cheese Croutons (page 125). Be sure to dollop the Four-Herb Pistou (page 27) on the tomatoes, too.

SERVES 4

4 boneless skinless chicken breasts
  (about 1 1/2 pounds/750 g)
Olive oil for brushing
Kosher or sea salt and
  freshly ground black pepper

2 lemons, halved
1 cup (250 ml) Four-Herb Pistou (page 27),
  prepared

Prepare a hot fire in your grill.

Place each chicken breast between two sheets of plastic wrap and pound to 1/2-inch (1 cm) thickness with a meat mallet or the edge of a sturdy saucer. Brush the chicken with olive oil and season with salt and pepper. Lightly brush lemon halves with olive oil, too. Grill the chicken for 2 1/2 minutes per side, turning once, or until the chicken is no longer pink inside. Grill the lemon halves, cut-side down, for about 3 to 4 minutes. Serve the chicken immediately, with a squeeze of lemon juice and a dollop of Four-Herb Pistou atop each paillard.

SPIT-ROASTED CHICKEN WITH CHARRED TOMATOES ON THE VINE

PARIS HAS SEVERAL WELL-KNOWN BISTROS THAT SPECIALIZE IN ROTISSERIE COOKing. La Rôtisserie d'en Face serves spit-roasted chicken and planked Dover sole. L'Atelier Maître Albert calls itself a "contemporary" rotisserie and offers spit-roasted chicken, veal shank, and beef roast along with planked cod and sea bream. Blogger and cookbook author David Lebovitz, who lives in Paris, recommends the spit-roasted chicken and game birds at La Rôtisserie du Beaujolais. So why not have a little Paris in your backyard? If you like, brush baby zucchini and pattypan squash with the Lemon-Parsley Baste to grill alongside the tomatoes on the vine to round out the meal—and create a beautiful presentation on the platter. Tomatoes on the vine from the grocery store are usually on the small side, so plan on two tomatoes per person when you are shopping. If you cannot find ground fennel seeds, grind your own in a spice grinder or pound with a meat mallet between two sheets of plastic wrap or parchment paper.

SERVES 8

Lemon-Parsley Baste

6 garlic cloves, minced

½ cup (125 ml) finely chopped fresh
    flat-leaf parsley

¼ cup (50 ml) freshly squeezed lemon juice

¼ cup (50 ml) olive oil

2 teaspoons ground fennel seeds

2 whole chickens (each 3 to 4 pounds/
    1.5 to 2 kg), giblets and necks removed

Kosher or sea salt and
    freshly ground black pepper

2 or 3 vines of tomatoes with at least
    16 tomatoes total (about 5 to 6 pounds/
    2.5 to 3 kg)

For the Lemon-Parsley Baste, whisk together the garlic, parsley, lemon juice, olive oil, and fennel in a bowl. Transfer half of the baste to another bowl; cover and refrigerate.

Place the chickens in a large dish and season inside and out with salt and pepper. Brush the chickens with half of the baste, coating evenly. Cover with plastic wrap and refrigerate for at least 30 minutes or up to 8 hours.

Meanwhile, prepare an indirect fire in your grill or set up your grill for rotisserie cooking (page 18).

Place the tomatoes on the vine on a baking sheet and brush with some of the reserved marinade.

Prepare the chicken by tying the legs together with soaked kitchen string.

For rotisserie grilling, attach the chickens to the spit, leaving about 6 inches (15 cm) between the birds. Heat the grill to medium-high. Close the lid and grill for 3 to 4 hours, basting with the reserved Lemon-Parsley Baste halfway through, until an instant-read thermometer inserted in the thickest part of a thigh registers 160°F (75°C) and the leg joint moves easily. Transfer chickens to serving platters, tent with foil, and let rest for 15 minutes.

Carve the chickens and arrange the pieces attractively on a platter. Surround with the grilled tomatoes on the vine.

VARIATION:

If you prefer, you can grill the chickens over a hot indirect fire instead of using the rotisserie. Place the chickens on the indirect side of the grill. Close the lid and grill for 3 to 4 hours, turning the chickens 180 degrees and basting with the reserved baste halfway through, until a meat thermometer inserted in the thickest part of thigh registers 160°F (75°C) and the leg joint moves easily.

PLANKED CHICKEN BREASTS WITH ARTICHOKE SLATHER

PLANKING BONELESS, SKINLESS CHICKEN BREASTS IS YET ANOTHER WAY TO DO something deliciously different with a common ingredient. Cooking on a plank produces chicken that is tender and juicy with the slight woodsy aroma of the plank. The Artichoke Slather keeps the chicken wonderfully moist. Make sure you soak your plank for at least 1 hour before you put it on the grill.

SERVES 4

4 boneless skinless chicken breasts

One 15 x 6½ x 8 inch (37 x 16 x 20 cm) cedar or oak plank, soaked in water for at least 1 hour

Kosher salt and freshly ground black pepper

1 recipe Artichoke Slather (page 28), prepared

Prepare an indirect medium-hot fire in your grill.

Place the chicken breasts on the water-soaked plank and lightly sprinkle with salt and pepper. Spread the slather over the chicken, sealing it around the edges of the plank. Bring the plank outside.

Place the plank on the indirect side of the grill. Close the grill lid and cook for about 20 minutes. Open the grill and turn the plank 180 degrees and close the grill lid again. Continue to cook for about another 20 minutes or until an instant-read meat thermometer inserted in the thickest part of the chicken breast registers 160°F (75°C). Serve hot.

VARIATIONS:

Slathers are a great way to keep tender cuts of meat moist. You can slather pork tenderloin or fish fillets. The other slathers in our book can be easily changed out for one another, so be sure to try the Shallot Slather, Caper Slather, or the combination of all the ingredients—our Artichoke-Shallot-Caper Slather (page 28).

MOROCCAN CHICKEN WITH APRICOT AND PISTACHIO COUSCOUS

WE HAVE THE FRENCH FOREIGN LEGION TO THANK FOR THE MOROCCAN INFLUENCE in bistro cuisine. Honey-sweet and savory with spice, this chicken dish is a meal in minutes. Just add a Green Salad (page 70). The marinade is multifunctional: One half flavors the chicken; the other half dresses the couscous. Here's looking at you, kid. It's always good to oil the grill rack well before heating up the grill, but it's especially important when you're grilling foods that have been marinated in a sweet mixture, so they don't stick.

SERVES 4

Moroccan Marinade

2 garlic cloves, minced

1 bunch green onions, chopped, about 1 cup (225 g)

1/2 cup (125 ml) dry white wine

3 tablespoons honey

2 tablespoons olive oil

2 teaspoons ground cumin

2 teaspoons ground coriander

1/2 teaspoon ground cinnamon

1 pound (450 g) boneless skinless chicken thighs

Apricot and Pistachio Couscous

1/2 cup (60 g) dried apricots, snipped into small pieces

1/2 cup (120 ml) hot water

1 2/3 cups (290 g) instant couscous

1/2 cup (60 g) shelled roasted pistachios

For the marinade, whisk together garlic, green onions, wine, honey, olive oil, cumin, coriander, and cinnamon in a bowl. Set aside.

Place the chicken in a large sealable plastic bag and pour in half the marinade. Seal, toss to coat, and refrigerate for at least 30 minutes or up to 8 hours, tossing occasionally. Cover and refrigerate the remaining marinade until ready to use.

Prepare a medium-hot fire in your grill.

For the Apricot and Pistachio Couscous, place the apricots in a small bowl, pour in hot water, and let soften for about 5 minutes. Prepare the couscous according to package directions. Drain the apricots. Toss the couscous with the reserved marinade, apricots, and pistachios. Set aside.

Remove the chicken from the marinade, discarding the marinade. Grill the chicken for 18 to 20 minutes, turning every 3 to 4 minutes, until the juices run clear when the chicken is pierced or until a meat thermometer inserted in the thickest part of thigh registers 160°F (75°C). Serve the chicken on a bed of Apricot and Pistachio Couscous.

BRIE AND TAPENADE–STUFFED CHICKEN BREAST

LET THIS RECIPE BE YOUR BLUEPRINT TO CREATE VARIATIONS: FRENCH FETA AND roasted red bell peppers, Cheddar cheese and bacon, and chopped green onions and Boursin cheese are all delicious stuffing alternatives. Serve sliced rounds of the stuffed chicken with a cold salad the next day. When ready to serve, cut into 1/4-inch (0.5-cm) slices and arrange on the salad of your choice.

SERVES 6

6 boneless, skinless chicken breasts, each about 4 to 6 ounces (125 to 175 g)

Six 1/4-inch (0.5-cm) slices Brie cheese

3 tablespoons Black Olive Tapenade (page 59)

Olive oil for brushing

Fennel Salt (page 24)

Freshly ground black pepper

3/4 cup Whole-Grain Mustard Sauce (page 34)

Prepare a medium-hot fire in your grill.

Slit a lengthwise pocket horizontally along the side of each chicken breast and stuff each with one slice of Brie and 1½ teaspoons tapenade. Lightly coat chicken with olive oil and season to taste with Fennel Salt and pepper.

Grill the chicken for 6 to 7 minutes per side, turning once, or until a meat thermometer inserted in the thickest part of a breast (but not in the stuffing) registers 160°F (75°C). Let rest for 5 minutes, and then slice into 1/2-inch-thick (1 cm) slices on the diagonal. Serve with the Whole-Grain Mustard Sauce on the side.

VARIATION:

Make roulades by pounding chicken breasts to 1/2 inch (1 cm) thick. Place Brie and tapenade down the center of each flattened chicken breast. Roll up and secure with soaked toothpicks. Grill for about the same amount of time, making sure to quarter turn the roulades every 3 to 4 minutes and closing the grill lid when not turning the chicken.

SPATCHCOCKED CHICKEN WITH ROSEMARY SPRIGS

THE FRENCH HAVE A VERY INELEGANT BUT DESCRIPTIVE WAY TO DESCRIBE SPATCH-cocked chicken. *Poulet en crapaudine* means chicken that is flattened like a toad. The chicken needs lots of grill attention, so prepare easy sides that you can make ahead like the Potato Gratin (page 98) or grill alongside the chicken like the Stir-Grilled Haricots Verts with Lemon Verbena Pistou (page 101).

SERVES 4 TO 6

1 whole chicken, 3½ to 4 pounds (1.75 to 2 kg)

Olive oil

2 lemons cut in half

Kosher or sea salt and
    freshly ground black pepper

¼ cup (60 ml) Provençal Herb Rub (page 22)

5 or 6 fresh rosemary branches,
    6 to 8 inches long (15 to 20 cm)

To spatchcock the chicken (or have your butcher do it), turn it breast-side down. With a pair of kitchen shears, cut along each side of the backbone, from neck to tail. Snip out the backbone completely. Also remove the wishbone. Turn the chicken breast-side up and press down to flatten. Place the flattened chicken in a large bowl and rub it all over with olive oil. Squeeze both lemons over the chicken, rubbing in the juice. Sprinkle with salt, pepper, and the Provençal Herb Rub. Marinate in the refrigerator, covered, for 2 to 3 hours.

Soak the rosemary branches in water to cover for at least 10 minutes (a little longer won't hurt). Weigh them down with a saucer, if necessary, to keep them submerged.

Prepare a hot fire in your grill.

When ready to grill, remove the chicken from the marinade. Remove the rosemary branches from the water and shake off the excess water. Place the branches on the hot grill in such a way that they won't fall through. Brush the underside of the chicken with a bit of olive oil and place skin-side up on top of the branches. Cover and cook for 10 to 15 minutes. Brush the chicken with olive oil and turn over so the skin side is against the rosemary. Cover and cook for another 10 to 15 minutes. If the chicken begins to turn too dark, pull it to the side of the grill briefly. If the rosemary begins to flame, remove it or spritz lightly with water. Continue to check and turn the chicken, brushing with more oil, if necessary, every 10 minutes or so until an instant-read meat thermometer inserted in the thickest part of the thigh (but not against the bone) registers 160°F (75°C), about 40 minutes total. Serve hot.

TARRAGON-INFUSED GRILLED TURKEY BREAST

TARRAGON VINEGAR ADDS LOTS OF TANGY FLAVOR TO THIS BIRD. YOU NEED TO TEND to the turkey during most of this grilling process, so serve with made-ahead side dishes like Garden Tomato Salad (page 70) or Barbecued White Beans with Bacon and Pear (page 102). Save some of the reserved marinade to dress shredded cabbage for a delicious slaw. When grilling or smoking two turkey breasts (or roasts or briskets), make sure both pieces weigh about the same, so that the cooking time will be similar.

SERVES 8 TO 10

Suggested wood: Oak, apple, or grapevines

Tarragon Vinegar Marinade

⅓ cup (75 ml) dry white wine

⅓ cup (75 ml) tarragon vinegar

⅓ cup (75 ml) peanut oil

1 tablespoon poultry seasoning

1 tablespoon freshly ground black pepper

2 teaspoons garlic salt

2 teaspoons dried tarragon

1 teaspoon hot pepper sauce

1 teaspoon freshly squeezed lemon juice

2 bone-in turkey breasts
(each about 4 pounds/2 kg)

1 handful dry wood chips

For the Tarragon Vinegar Marinade, whisk together the wine, vinegar, peanut oil, poultry seasoning, pepper, garlic salt, tarragon, hot pepper sauce, and lemon juice in a bowl.

Place the turkey in a sealable plastic bag and pour in half the marinade. Seal, toss to coat, and refrigerate for at least 30 minutes or up to 8 hours, turning occasionally. Cover and refrigerate the remaining marinade until ready to use.

Meanwhile, prepare an indirect hot fire with a kiss of smoke (page 15) in your grill and add your desired type of wood. (Replenish the wood chips or grapevines as necessary.)

Remove the turkey from the marinade, discarding marinade. When you see the first wisp of smoke from the wood, place the turkey breasts on the direct or hot side of the grill. Grill for 30 to 45 minutes, turning and basting with the reserved marinade every 5 minutes, then transfer the turkey breasts to the indirect side of the grill and close the grill lid. Smoke-roast for another 15 to 20 minutes or until a meat thermometer inserted in the thickest part of a breast registers 160°F (75°C). Let rest for 5 minutes before carving.

CHAPTER 9

AGNEAU
LAMB

Bistro lamb dishes go one of two ways—cooked hot and fast to a rare or medium-rare finish, or slow-cooked to fall-apart tenderness.

You can get the same results, but with decidedly more flavor, on your grill.

Take the classic bistro dish, a leg of lamb or *gigot* served with white beans or *flageolets*. Both get an extra smoky oomph from the grill, so they go back in time to the original hearth recipe of French home cooks. What goes around, comes around.

A boned and butterflied leg of lamb, marinated in an herby mixture like Four-Herb Pistou (page 27), gets charry on the outside but stays moist and pink on the inside.

Lamb chops—as paillards, thick chops, or rack of lamb—pair well with the piquant sauces that the French do so well—Béarnaise Sauce (page 36), Sauce Paloise (page 36), and Mustard-Cornichon Beurre Blanc (page 38).

GRILLED LAMB CHOPS, PAILLARD-STYLE

A PAILLARD IS BASICALLY A CUTLET—A BONELESS, SKINLESS PIECE OF CHICKEN OR meat that is pounded to a uniform thinness so it cooks quickly, bistro-style, over a hot fire. You can also make a paillard from a bone-in lamb chop—just pound the boneless part until it is ½ inch (1 cm) thick, leaving the bone intact. A squeeze of lemon and a drizzle of extra-virgin olive oil after grilling would be a simple and delicious finish to this dish, but a dollop or two of Sauce Paloise (variation, page 36), Béarnaise Sauce (page 36), Lime-Cilantro Remoulade (page 32), or Avocado Crème Fraîche (page 33) would add a certain *je ne sais quoi*, as well. If you like, grill asparagus along with the lamb and serve them both with a sauce of your choice.

SERVES 8

12 lamb loin or shoulder chops
   (about 2 pounds/1 kg), pounded
   to ½-inch (1-cm) thickness
Olive oil for brushing

Rosemary Salt (page 24)
Lemon wedges and fresh rosemary branches,
   for garnish

Prepare a hot fire in your grill.

Brush the lamb with olive oil and season with Rosemary Salt. Grill for 1 to 2 minutes per side, turning once, until medium-rare, or until your desired doneness. Garnish with lemon wedges and rosemary branches and serve right away.

THICK LITTLE LAMB CHOPS
WITH MUSTARD–CORNICHON BEURRE BLANC

THICK LITTLE LAMB CHOPS MAKE A MEAL WITH ACCOMPANIMENTS LIKE SIMPLE grilled fingerling potatoes and maybe a Smoked Goat Cheese Salad with Sweet Cherries (page 77). For bigger appetites, you might want to serve two of these chops per person. Prepare the Mustard-Cornichon Beurre Blanc (page 38) a day or so ahead of time.

SERVES 4 TO 8

8 thick boneless lamb loin chops, about 1½ pounds (750 g)

Olive oil for brushing

Kosher or sea salt and freshly ground black pepper

1 recipe Mustard-Cornichon Beurre Blanc (page 38), prepared

Lemon wedges and fresh rosemary branches, for garnish

Prepare a hot fire in your grill.

Brush the lamb with olive oil and season with salt and pepper. Grill for 2 to 3 minutes per side, turning once, until medium-rare, or until desired doneness.

Serve with Mustard-Cornichon Beurre Blanc. Garnish with lemon wedges and rosemary branches.

VARIATION:

Think outside of the box and use these delicious little chops as the meat for a composed Salad Niçoise (instead of the traditional tuna). You'll need lettuce, tomatoes, Niçoise (cured) olives, hard-boiled eggs, and new potatoes; dress with the Lemon-Tarragon Vinaigrette (page 26). *Formidable!*

GRILLED LAMB STEAK WITH SAUCE PALOISE

A HOT FIRE AND THIN LAMB STEAKS, PROVENÇAL ROSÉ WINE, A WARM LOAF OF crusty bread, Provençal Grill-Roasted Tomatoes (page 108) or Planked Goat Cheese–Topped Beefsteak Tomatoes (page 107), and you'll have a fresh-tasting, summery meal to remember. Sauce Paloise is a version of the classic béarnaise, made with mint instead of tarragon.

SERVES 4

4 boneless lamb leg steaks (about 1½ pounds/375 g), cut about ¾ inch (2 cm) thick

Olive oil for brushing

Kosher or sea salt and freshly ground black pepper

1 recipe Sauce Paloise (variation, page 36), prepared

Prepare a hot fire in your grill.

Brush the lamb steaks with olive oil and season to taste with salt and pepper. Grill for 2 minutes per side, turning once, until medium-rare, or until desired doneness. Serve with the Sauce Paloise.

GRILLING SAVOIR FAIRE: BISTRO LAMB CUTS AND THE BEST BARBECUE METHODS

For the best-tasting lamb, grill it hot and fast so that it reaches a doneness of rare or medium-rare, or go low and slow with a kiss of smoke. Tougher or thicker cuts of lamb benefit from lower and slower cooking, while thin, tender cuts benefit from high-heat direct grilling.

Breast or shoulder	Smoke/braise
Boneless meat	Smoke/braise
Burger	Grill
Chops	Grill
Leg of lamb	Grill, rotisserie, smoke
Rack of lamb	Grill, indirect grill, grill with kiss of smoke
Steak	Grill

LAVENDER-SMOKED RACK OF LAMB

SMOLDERING LAVENDER STICKS, CUT FROM THE PLANT IN LATE SUMMER, ADD EVEN more aromatic flavor to rack of lamb on the grill. We use lavender cut from our gardens, but you can also use any aromatic, woody herb such as rosemary, thyme, fennel, or even grapevines. Ask your butcher to French the racks of lamb for the grill. This process removes excess fat from the bones, and some from the meat, too. Plan ahead and pop a Potato Gratin (page 98) in the oven ahead of time, toss a salad of baby greens, warm a baguette (wrapped in foil) on the grill, and dinner is served!

SERVES 2 TO 4

Suggested wood: Dried lavender sticks, fennel stalks, or grapevines

2 racks of lamb (each about 1½ pounds/750g), fat removed and bones Frenched

1 recipe Herbes de Provence Flavoring Paste (page 28)

Slather the lamb with the flavoring paste and set aside.

Prepare a hot indirect fire with a kiss of smoke (page 15) in your grill and add your desired type of wood.

Place lamb over the fire and sear on all sides. Transfer to the indirect side of the grill. When the lavender starts to smolder, close the lid and grill for 15 to 20 minutes, until a meat thermometer inserted in the thickest part of a rack registers 130°F (54°C) for medium-rare, or until desired doneness. Transfer to a cutting board, tent with foil, and let rest for 10 minutes before slicing.

GRILLED LEG OF LAMB PISTOU
WITH MEDITERRANEAN VEGETABLES AND AIOLI

THIS CELEBRATORY LEG OF LAMB BATHES IN PISTOU BEFORE IT SEARS ON THE grill. The mixture of vegetables grills right along with the lamb. Then it's all finished off with garlicky Food Processor Aioli (page 29) and served on big white platters, true bistro-style.

SERVES 8

1 boned and butterflied leg of lamb,
  3 to 4 pounds/1.5 to 2 kg

1 recipe Four-Herb Pistou (page 27), prepared

2 pounds (1 kg) Japanese or baby eggplant

4 large red, yellow, green, or orange bell
  peppers, cored, seeded, and quartered

2 large red onions (about 2 pounds/1 kg), peeled
  and cut into 1-inch-thick (2.5 cm) slices

Olive oil for brushing

Kosher or sea salt and
  freshly ground black pepper

Chopped fresh flat-leaf parsley, for garnish

1 recipe Food Processor Aioli (page 29),
  prepared

Place the lamb in an extra-large sealable plastic bag. Add the Four-Herb Pistou. Seal the bag, toss to coat, and refrigerate at least 4 hours and up to 24 hours, tossing occasionally.

Prepare a medium-hot fire in your grill.

Brush the vegetables with the olive oil and season with salt and pepper.

Remove the lamb from the marinade and pat dry. Discard the marinade and the bag. Place the lamb over direct heat and grill for 15 minutes per side or until a thermometer inserted in the thickest part of the lamb registers 125 to 130°F (48 to 50°C) for medium-rare. Let the lamb rest for 10 minutes before slicing. Grill the vegetables until blistered and softened, turning often, about 20 minutes. To serve, place the lamb slices on a platter surrounded by the vegetables. Garnish all with chopped parsley. Spoon the aioli into a serving bowl and a bowl pass around to everyone at the table.

SMOKY LAMB DAUBE

FALL-APART TENDER, THIS LAMB HAS THE ANCIENT FLAVOR OF THE INDOOR hearth, but it is prepared outside on the grill or smoker. We use the same technique in Provençal Beef Daube (page 170), with good-sized chunks of meat and red wine, which typifies a French *daube* (or stew). Use a good-quality (but not expensive) dry red wine, such as Cabernet, Pinot Noir, or Burgundy. Do not overcrowd the pan when browning the lamb, or it will not brown properly. Instead of the foil pans, you could use an old pot that you don't mind getting smoke-stained. Place the foil pans or the pot on a large baking sheet to take out to the grill, as it is easier to carry this way. For contrast, serve this with one of the Simple Bistro Salads *à Deux* (page 70) or the Bistro Grated Carrot Salad (page 73) or Celery Root Remoulade (page 71) made with grated fresh vegetables. Serve the Smoky Lamb Daube over mashed potatoes, polenta, or Barbecued White Beans with Bacon and Pear (page 102), which you could put on the grill at the same time as the lamb.

SERVES 8

2 large heavy-duty foil pans (doubled up to use as one pan) or an old, large pot with a lid

Suggested wood: Apple and/or oak

3 tablespoons olive oil (approximately)

3 pounds (1.5 g) boneless lamb shoulder, cut into 2-inch (5-cm) cubes

2 tablespoons water

3 sprigs fresh thyme

2 shallots, diced

1 (3-ounce/90-g) carrot, diced

1 small stalk celery, diced

1 head garlic, cloves separated and peeled

2 tablespoons all-purpose flour

1 bottle (3 cups/750 ml) medium- to full-bodied dry red wine

1 teaspoon red wine vinegar

Additional fresh thyme sprigs, for garnish (optional)

In a wide-bottomed pot, heat the olive oil over medium-high heat until smoking. Using paper towels, blot moisture from the chunks of lamb to help it brown better. Working in batches, sauté the lamb for 8 to 10 minutes, or until browned on all sides, adding oil as necessary between batches. Transfer the lamb to the doubled foil pans.

Add the water to the pot, scraping up any browned bits from the bottom. Pour the pan juices into the foil pan. Stir in the thyme, shallots, carrot, celery, and garlic. Whisk in the flour, and then stir in the wine.

Prepare an indirect fire with a kiss of smoke in your grill (page 15) and add your desired type of wood. (Replenish the wood chips as necessary.)

Place the pan on the indirect side of the grill. When you see the first wisp of smoke, close the lid and smoke for 1 hour. Stir, cover with foil, close the lid, and smoke for another hour, or until the lamb is fork-tender. Using a slotted spoon, remove the lamb to a platter and keep warm.

Transfer the contents of the pan to a food processor or blender, discarding the thyme, and purée. Stir in the vinegar. Pour the sauce over the lamb and garnish with thyme sprigs, if desired.

VARIATION:

Any type of shoulder meat, such as beef chuck or pork shoulder blade (butt), can be cooked this way. Just smoke until fork-tender. You can also cook the lamb *daube*, covered, in a 350°F (180°C) oven, then put it on the grill, uncovered, for the last hour or so.

VIANDE DE GIBIER
GAME

In France, hunting is a way of country life, and the lineages of hunting dogs can be traced for hundreds of years. Until the French Revolution, hunting was the preserve of the rich and the royal. When we were at Chateau du Fey in Burgundy, one of our day trips was to the International Museum of the Hunt in Gien, where rifles and guns, oil portraits of prized hunting dogs, and still-life paintings with game as the centerpiece held our interest. The still-life art of French painters such as Jean Siméon Chardin and Jean-Baptiste Oudry (widely exhibited in the Louvre and major museums throughout the world) celebrate the bounty of the wild and the skill of the hunter.

So does this chapter.

Prized game meat cooked properly is nothing less than wonderful. Without hormones, all natural, and forage-fed in the wild, game such as elk, deer, wild boar, ducks, geese, pheasant, grouse, and squab all have unique, fuller flavors than domestic game. Most game meat is very lean with little fat to marble it. Because of that, it is best to cook game meat quickly over higher heat to about medium-rare to medium. This makes game a perfect choice for the high heat of the grill.

There are also other things that hunters bring home after *la chasse*. That could be wild mushrooms and blackberries foraged along the way, or even frog legs. If it's local and wild, the hunter will find it.

WOOD-FIRED DUCK BREASTS WITH FRESH HERB BUTTER

WILD MALLARD DUCK BREASTS ARE VERY SMALL, ABOUT 6 OUNCES (175 G). Domestic Muscovy or Long Island duck breasts are about 8 ounces (250 g), while moulard duck breasts can weigh up to 1 pound (500 g)! If you use large duck breasts, grill them longer, with your meat thermometer at the ready. You're aiming for 145°F (65°C) for medium at the most.

SERVES 4

Suggested wood: Apple, cherry, orange, or pear fruitwood

4 boneless skinless mallard duck breasts

1 tablespoon olive oil

1 teaspoon coarse kosher salt

1 teaspoon freshly cracked black peppercorns

½ cup (113 g) Fresh Herb Butter (page 47)

4 slices of baguette

Using a meat mallet, pound the duck breast to ¾-inch (2-cm) thickness. Lightly coat with olive oil and sprinkle with salt and pepper. Set Aside.

Prepare a medium-hot fire with a kiss of smoke (page 15) in your grill.

Grill the duck for 2½ to 3 minutes per side, turning once, until a meat thermometer inserted in the thickest part of a breast registers 140°F (60°C) for medium-rare, or until desired doneness. Transfer to a cutting board, tent with foil, and let rest for 5 minutes before slicing. Spread some of the extra herb butter on the slices of bread. Slice the duck breasts and fan onto each plate. Top with a dollop of herb butter and serve with the herb-buttered bread on the side.

VARIATION:

For a more casual recipe, make duck croissant sandwiches. Slather with the spread of your choice or a drizzle of the Port Cherry Sauce (page 175). Place a grilled duck breast on each roll and top with thin slice of red onion and crumbled French feta or Roquefort blue cheese.

THE ARMCHAIR HUNTER'S GUIDE TO GAME MEATS

If you don't hunt but still would like to try game meats, where can you find them? You can try specialty butcher shops or Dean & Deluca. D'Artagnan, founded by Ariane Daguin in upstate New York, is the Francophile's go-to source for duck, pheasant, venison, rabbit, wild boar, and more at www.dartagnan.com. Broken Arrow Ranch in Texas offers venison, wild boar, and antelope at www.brokenarrowranch.com.

CAMEMBERT-STUFFED
AND PROSCIUTTO-WRAPPED PHEASANT BREASTS

THE KEY TO SMOKING IS NOT LOOKING. WHEN YOU OPEN THE LID TO TAKE A PEEK, the heat escapes and you'll need to add 5 to 10 minutes to compensate. The smoke also escapes . . . so don't peek. The Camembert will soften and begin to ooze out of the breasts while they cook, but the foil pan will keep the melting cheese from falling into the grill.

SERVES 4

Suggested wood: Oak, apple, maple, pecan, or chestnut

4 boneless skinless pheasant breasts (about 6 to 7 ounces/175 to 205 g each)

4 ounces (125 g) Camembert, sliced

8 basil leaves

4 slices prosciutto

2 tablespoons olive oil

Prepare an indirect fire with a kiss of smoke (page 15) in your grill and add your desired type of wood.

Using a meat mallet, pound the pheasant to ½-inch (1-cm) thickness. Place on a work surface, smooth-side down. Place 1 ounce (30 g) of Camembert and two basil leaves in the middle of each breast. Fold the side over (like an omelet) to enclose the cheese and basil, tucking a little bit of the ends inward, too. Wrap each with a slice of prosciutto and lightly coat with olive oil. Place in foil pan.

Place the foil pan on the indirect side of the grill. Close the lid and smoke for 45 to 55 minutes, or until a meat thermometer inserted in the thickest part of the breast registers 155°F (73°C). Transfer to a cutting board, tent with foil and let rest for 10 minutes. (The internal temperature of the breast meat will rise another 5°F [2°C] for a perfect well-done breast). Slice crosswise into slightly less than 1-inch-thick (2.5 cm) slices.

VARIATION:
Pounding the pheasant breast is a way to slightly tenderize the meat. If you know the pheasant is young (and tender), then you may simply slit the breast to make a pocket, stuff the pocket with the cheese and herbs, and then wrap in the prosciutto. Other stuffing combinations like apricots, pistachios, and Brie; tapenade and goat cheese; or feta and chives would be equally delicious.

HERB-GRILLED RABBIT
WITH WHOLE-GRAIN MUSTARD SAUCE

SOAKING WILD RABBIT IN MILK IS A COMMON MARINADE THAT IS SAID TO LESSEN the gaminess. If the rabbit is domestic, no presoaking is necessary. You may also slather the rabbit with Herbes de Provence Flavoring Paste (page 28) instead of soaking. Serve the rabbit on a platter on top of Toasted Barley Pilaf with Grilled Garden Vegetables (page 121).

SERVES 4

Suggested wood: Apple, cherry, oak, or pecan

1 wild or domestic rabbit (about 3 pounds/
    1.5 kg), cut into 8 pieces

2 cups (500 ml) milk (optional)

2 tablespoons olive oil

2 tablespoons Provençal Herb Rub
    (page 22), prepared

1 cup (250 ml) Whole-Grain Mustard Sauce
    (page 34), prepared

If using wild rabbit, place the pieces in a large bowl and add the milk. Cover and refrigerate for at least 4 hours or overnight. Remove the rabbit from the milk, discard the milk, and pat the rabbit dry.

Place the rabbit pieces in a shallow dish, rub with olive oil, and sprinkle with the Provençal Herb Rub. Cover and refrigerate for 2 hours.

Meanwhile, prepare a medium-hot fire with a kiss of smoke (page 15) in your grill and add your desired type of wood.

When you see the first wisp of smoke from the wood, place rabbit on the grill. Close the lid and grill for 8 to 10 minutes per side, turning once, until a meat thermometer inserted in the thickest part of a rabbit piece registers 160°F (75°C). Serve with Whole-Grain Mustard Sauce.

VARIATION:

In a hurry? If the preparation of the rub and the sauce are daunting because you don't have time or just don't want to make them, simply substitute herbes de Provence or dried crushed rosemary for the rub and use whole-grain mustard for the sauce.

VENISON TENDERLOIN
WITH BLACKBERRY BRANDY BEURRE BLANC

VENISON TENDERLOIN, CHOPS, AND STEAKS ARE COVETED CUTS FROM DEER AND elk. If you don't have time to make the sauce, simply grill them with the olive oil, salt, and pepper. But once you taste the sauce you'll find time to make it. This sauce is also wonderful paired with grilled duck breast.

SERVES 4

Blackberry Brandy Beurre Blanc

1 garlic clove, minced

1 cup (250 ml) blackberry brandy

1/4 cup (50 ml) freshly squeezed lemon juice

1 tablespoon minced shallot

1 cup (250 ml) heavy whipping cream

1/4 cup (56 g) cold unsalted butter,
    cut into pieces

1 cup (125 g) fresh or
    frozen blackberries, thawed

2 pounds (1 kg) deer or elk tenderloin
    or 8 chops (each about 4 ounces/125 g
    and 1/2 inch/1 cm thick)

Olive oil for brushing

Coarse kosher salt and
    freshly cracked black peppercorns

For the Blackberry Brandy Beurre Blanc, combine the garlic, brandy, lemon juice, and shallots in a small saucepan. Bring to a boil over medium-high heat. Continue to boil, stirring often, until it is reduced to about 1/4 cup (50 ml), about 5 minutes. Add the cream and return to a boil. Boil until the sauce is reduced by half, about 5 minutes. Remove from the heat and whisk in the butter, one piece at a time, whisking until the sauce glistens and thickens. Stir in the blackberries and keep warm.

Prepare a hot fire in your grill.

Lightly brush the venison tenderloin or chops with olive oil and season to taste with salt and pepper. Grill the tenderloin for 5 minutes per side, turning once, until medium-rare, or until desired doneness. Grill the chops for about 2 minutes per side, turning once, until medium-rare, or until desired doneness. Remove the tenderloin or chops from the heat and tent with foil for about 10 minutes to let the meat rest. To serve, slice the tenderloin at a 45-degree angle. Spoon the Blackberry Brandy Beurre Blanc over the sliced tenderloin or the chops and serve.

GRILLED FROG LEGS
WITH GARLIC AND WHITE WINE

A GARLIC AND WHITE WINE SAUCE IS THE CLASSIC BISTRO PREPARATION FOR FROG legs. We stay true to that sauce, but we grill the frog legs for a wonderful charred flavor. Nothing else is needed with this recipe except for a good loaf of crusty bread. You can find frog legs at specialty butcher shops or seafood shops or online.

SERVES 4

2 pounds (1 kg) frog legs, cleaned and skinned

1 cup (250 ml) olive oil

1 cup (250 ml) dry white wine

1/4 cup (50 ml) chopped fresh flat-leaf parsley

4 garlic cloves, minced

Zest and juice of 2 lemons,
    plus 2 additional lemons

1/4 cup (56 g) butter

Kosher or sea salt and
    freshly ground black pepper

1 loaf of crusty French or Italian bread, sliced,
    and wrapped in foil

Place the frog legs in a large sealable plastic bag. Combine the olive oil, wine, parsley, garlic, lemon zest, and lemon juice. Pour half of the mixture into the bag of frog legs and refrigerate for 24 hours. Reserve the rest of the marinade in a separate container and refrigerate.

When ready to grill, prepare a medium-hot fire in your grill.

Pour the reserved marinade into a saucepan and bring to a boil. Reduce heat to a simmer and add the butter. Keep warm.

Place the frog legs on a baking sheet and season with salt and pepper. Cut the remaining lemons in half. Take out to the grill with the foil-wrapped bread.

Grill the frog legs over the fire for about 3 minutes per side. Grill the lemon halves for about 2 minutes, cut-side down. Place the foil-wrapped bread in the back of the grill and warm it while the frog legs and lemon halves are grilling.

Arrange the grilled frog legs on a platter and pour the warm marinade over all. Serve with the grilled lemon halves for those who like another squeeze of lemon on the frog legs and a basket of the crusty bread for mopping up the sauce.

VARIATION:

If you start with the basic marinade recipe above, you can add 2 or 3 tablespoons of soy sauce for an Asian-flavored marinade. Instead of the parsley, use chives or cilantro for an additional flavor change.

GRILLED WILD BOAR STEAKS WITH STIR-GRILLED APPLES

IN THE FALL, BISTRO MENUS OFFER WILD BOAR OR *MARCASSIN*, USUALLY AS A SLOW-cooked dish. Our grilled version is also delicious, benefitting from another seasonal favorite, apples. The wild boar steaks are from the loin and are also referred to as chops. This is the tenderest meat and can be grilled, much like hanger or flank steak, to your desired doneness (but optimally, rare). You can find wild boar at specialty butchers or online at shops such as www.brokenarrowranch.com.

SERVES 6

Stir-Grilled Apples

2 tablespoons packed brown sugar

1 tablespoon coarse kosher salt

1 tablespoon red pepper flakes

1 tablespoon freshly cracked black peppercorns

½ teaspoon ground cloves

4 garlic cloves, minced

4 tablespoons olive oil

6 apples, crisp tart varieties like Jonagold

6 (8-ounce/250-g) wild boar steaks or chops

Prepare a hot fire in your grill. Lightly oil a grill wok or basket.

For the Stir-Grilled Apples, combine the brown sugar, salt, pepper flakes, cracked pepper, and cloves, whisking to combine. Stir in the garlic and olive oil.

Core and quarter the apples and place in a bowl. Spoon a third of the brown sugar mixture over the apples, stirring to coat the apples evenly, prior to grilling.

Coat the chops with the rest of the brown sugar mixture.

Grill the chops to 130°F (55°C) for rare and 140°F (60°C) for medium-rare. While the chops are grilling, place the apples in a grill wok. Toss with wooden spoons until apples are a bit browned and warmed through. Serve the chops in the center of a platter surrounded by the apples.

BOEUF
BEEF

Bistro beef dishes go one of two ways—cooked quickly, or very, very slowly.

The quick way involves steak cooked over a hot fire, from the classic Steak Frites (page 166) to Creole Coffee–Rubbed Filet Mignon with Béarnaise Sauce (page 163) and Grilled Rib-Eye Steak au Poivre with Onion Straws (page 164).

Perhaps no dish illustrates "BBQ bistro" better than the Provençal Beef Daube (page 170), in which the beef smokes first, then is marinated, and finally braised to fork tenderness.

CREOLE COFFEE–RUBBED FILET MIGNON WITH BÉARNAISE SAUCE

THE CREOLE COFFEE RUB GIVES A NEW ORLEANS FRENCH QUARTER TWIST TO THIS recipe for grilled filet mignon. Then we go classic and pair the coffee-rubbed steak with a luscious Béarnaise Sauce for a special dinner. Grill asparagus along with this, bake a Potato Gratin (page 98) ahead of time, and all you need is an elegant tart or a flourless chocolate cake for dessert. As you let the steaks rest, the internal temperature will go up 10 degrees, so keep that in mind as you grill. You can always put an under-done filet mignon back on the grill, but you can't rescue one that is over-cooked.

SERVES 8

Creole Coffee Rub

2 tablespoons finely ground chicory coffee
   or espresso

1 tablespoon Spanish paprika

1 tablespoon dark brown sugar

1 teaspoon dry mustard

2 teaspoons fine kosher or sea salt

2 teaspoons cayenne pepper

1 teaspoon freshly ground black pepper

1 teaspoon freshly ground white pepper

1 teaspoon dried tarragon

1 teaspoon dried oregano

4 (8-ounce/250-g) boneless filet mignon,
   rib-eye, sirloin, or strip steaks,
   cut 3/4 to 1 inch (1.5 to 2.5 cm) thick

Olive oil for brushing

1 recipe Béarnaise Sauce (page 36),
   prepared and kept warm

Prepare a hot fire in your grill.

Make the Creole Coffee Rub in a small bowl by combining the coffee, paprika, brown sugar, mustard, salt, cayenne, black and white peppers, tarragon, and oregano. Stir to blend and set aside.

Brush the steaks lightly with olive oil and season on both sides with the rub. Grill the steaks, covered, for 3 minutes on each side for medium-rare, 130°F (50°C). Serve each steak with a spoonful or two of the Béarnaise Sauce.

GRILLED RIB-EYE STEAK AU POIVRE WITH ONION STRAWS

ADD A SIDE OF CREAMED SPINACH AND YOU'VE GOT THE CLASSIC STEAKHOUSE entrée with a bistro twist! Steakhouses have commercial equipment that cranks out the BTUs for high, high heat, but you can achieve a charry exterior and tender, juicy interior by heating your grill very hot. To do so, heat with the lid closed. Then grill the steaks with the lid closed except for when you turn the steaks. Use a mandoline slicer for paper-thin onion slivers. You can fry the onion slivers earlier in the day and simply warm the slivers in a 350°F (180°C) oven, uncovered on a baking sheet, for about 10 minutes or until warmed through.

SERVES 4

Fried Onion Slivers

1 large onion, sliced paper-thin

$1/2$ cup (65 g) all-purpose flour

3 cups (750 ml) peanut oil

Kosher or sea salt

Four 8-ounce (250-g) rib-eye steaks, $1^{1}/2$ inches (4 cm) thick

Olive oil for brushing

3 tablespoons Three-Peppercorn Rub (page 23), prepared

1 teaspoon kosher or sea salt

1 recipe Three Peppercorn-Beurre Blanc (page 39), prepared

For the Fried Onion Slivers, toss the onion in flour until well coated. In a deep saucepan or an electric skillet, heat the peanut oil over medium heat until it registers 350°F (180°C) on a candy or deep-fry thermometer. Add the onion, in batches, and fry, stirring frequently, for 7 to 8 minutes, or until golden. Remove with a slotted spoon to a plate lined with paper towels. Season with salt. Set aside and keep warm.

Prepare a hot fire in your grill.

Brush the steaks with olive oil and sprinkle the peppercorn rub and the salt on both sides, pressing it into the steak. Grill for 2 to 3 minutes per side, with the grill lid closed, turning once, until charred with good grill marks on the outside and a meat thermometer inserted in the thickest part of a steak registers 130°F (50°C) for medium-rare, or until desired doneness. Serve the steaks with a side of the onion straws and spoon the Three-Peppercorn Beurre Blanc generously over the steaks.

BISTRO STEAK AND FRITES
WITH SHALLOT BUTTER

FRENCH BISTRO DINERS ARE PARTIAL TO HAVING THEIR STEAKS A LITTLE ON THE chewy side but very flavorful. For that type of steak, you want *bavette*, flat iron, hanger, or flank steak. *Bavette*, cut from the flank, can be found at specialty butcher shops or online at Niman Ranch. The flat iron steak is cut from chuck. Hanger steak, also cut from the flank, is actually a whole muscle and is chewier than flank steak; it's known in France as *onglet*. You need to tenderize these steaks either by marinating them for at least an hour (preferably 8 hours) or pounding them with a meat tenderizer or mallet. Then you grill them over a hot fire to medium-rare. The final crucial step is slicing them properly to serve. Cut the meat against the grain, on the diagonal, holding your knife at a 45-degree angle (so it's slanted, not straight up and down).

SERVES 4

Bavette Marinade

2 garlic cloves, minced

2 tablespoons olive oil

2 tablespoons red wine vinegar

2 tablespoons chopped fresh flat-leaf parsley

1½ pounds (750 g) beef bavette
or flank, hangar, or flat iron steak

Kosher or sea salt and
freshly ground black pepper

1 recipe Shallot Butter (page 47),
prepared, at soft room temperature

1 recipe Homemade Frites (page 167), prepared

8 ounces (250 g) fresh watercress or
mâche greens

For the Bavette Marinade, place the ingredients in a sealable plastic bag. Add the steak, seal the bag, and coat the steak with marinade. Refrigerate for at least 1 hour or up to 8 hours.

Prepare a hot fire in your grill.

Remove the meat from the marinade and pat dry. Season with salt and pepper.

Grill for 2 to 3 minutes per side for medium-rare. Remove to a platter and dot with half the Shallot Butter. Tent the meat with foil and let rest for 5 minutes. Cut against the grain, on the diagonal and at a 45-degree angle, into slices about ¼ inch (0.5 cm) thick. Serve warm with the remaining Shallot Butter, Homemade Frites, and watercress.

HOMEMADE FRITES

Basically, these are homemade French fries, but they sound better as frites, don't they? On bistro menus, you'll often find mussels (see Pan-Grilled Mussels on page 42) and thin, chewy steaks served with frites. The secrets to great frites include cutting them thin and keeping the oil at or around 350°F (180°C). A deep fryer is great, but you can also use an electric skillet or a deep skillet and a candy thermometer.

Serves 6 to 8

4 large Idaho potatoes, peeled (about 2 pounds/1 kg)
Vegetable oil such as peanut oil for frying
Coarse kosher or sea salt

Cut the potatoes lengthwise into ¼-inch-thick (0.5 cm) slices, and then cut each slice into ¼-inch-wide (5 cm) strips. Place the strips in a bowl of ice water for 15 minutes.

Drain the water from the potatoes and pat very dry with paper towels.

Add 2 inches (5 cm) of vegetable oil to a deep fryer or skillet. If using a skillet, place over medium-high heat. When the oil reaches 350°F (180°C), place half the potatoes in the hot oil and cook, turning if necessary, until the potatoes turn golden brown, 5 to 7 minutes. Transfer to paper towels and season with salt. Keep warm in a low oven 200°F (100°C) while you prepare the second batch. Serve immediately.

VARIATIONS:

Season the frites with Rosemary Salt or Fennel Salt (page 24) for a savory twist.

Some frites aficionados swear by double frying the potatoes. To do this, fry them the first time as above and drain on paper towels. Then fry them again for a few minutes until light golden brown. Keep warm until ready to serve them or serve them right away.

GRILLED SIRLOIN WITH ASPARAGUS, ONIONS, AND ROQUEFORT SAUCE

APLATTER OF FRESH TOMATOES AND SOME GOOD BREAD TO MOP UP THE SAUCE ARE all you need to complete this meal. A 2-pound (1 kg) sirloin, grilled rare or *bleu*, will also yield leftovers for future meals, another plus.

SERVES 4

Roquefort Sauce
Makes about 1⅓ cups (325 ml)

4 ounces (113 g) unsalted butter, melted

¼ cup (50 ml) Worcestershire sauce

6 ounces (175 g) Roquefort, Gorgonzola, or other blue cheese, crumbled

1 garlic clove, minced

Fine kosher or sea salt and freshly ground black pepper

3 tablespoons olive oil

3 large garlic cloves, minced

1 teaspoon dried or 1 tablespoon fresh rosemary leaves

1 boneless sirloin steak, 1½ to 2 pounds/750 g to 1 kg, cut 2 inches (5 cm) thick

1 pound (450 g) fresh asparagus, trimmed

2 large (1 pound/500 g) red onions, peeled and cut into 1-inch-thick (2.5 cm) slices

Olive oil for brushing

Fine kosher or sea salt and freshly ground pepper

Prepare a hot fire in your grill.

For the Roquefort Sauce, whisk the melted butter, Worcestershire sauce, Roquefort, garlic, and salt and pepper to taste together in a small bowl and set aside.

Mix the olive oil, garlic, and rosemary into a paste and spread over the surface of the meat. Brush the asparagus and onion slices with olive oil and season with salt and pepper to taste.

Grill the steak for 8 minutes, turning once, or until it registers 125°F (45°C) for rare, or until desired doneness. Remove the steak from the grill and let the meat rest for 5 minutes. Place the onions on the grill along with the steak. Turn the onions once after about 4 minutes or until they have softened and have good grill marks. Place the asparagus on a perforated grill rack and grill, turning often, until softened and browned. To serve, slice the steak on the diagonal, nap with the sauce, and accompany with the asparagus and onion.

GRILL-ROASTED TENDERLOIN
WITH BACON MUSHROOM SAUCE

GRILL THE TENDERLOIN WITH A LITTLE CHAR ON THE EXTERIOR, LEAVING THE interior rosy and juicy. You'll need a really hot fire, preferably one made with mesquite charcoal, though you can still have a very good tenderloin on a gas grill.

SERVES 10 TO 12

Suggested wood: A mixture of apple and oak
or cherry and pecan

Bacon Mushroom Sauce

12 ounces (375 g) thick-sliced bacon

4 ounces (125 g) mushrooms, sliced

1¹/₂ cups (375 g) sour cream

2 tablespoons finely chopped
fresh flat-leaf parsley

1 tablespoon grated onion

2 teaspoons prepared horseradish

1 beef tenderloin (6 to 8 pounds/
3 to 4 kg), trimmed

3 tablespoons melted unsalted butter

Coarse kosher salt and
freshly ground black pepper

For the Bacon Mushroom Sauce, fry the bacon in a large skillet until crisp. Transfer the bacon to a plate lined with paper towels. Pour off all but 2 tablespoons of the bacon fat and sauté the mushrooms until softened, 3 to 5 minutes. Transfer the mushrooms to a bowl and let cool. Crumble the bacon and add to bowl of mushrooms. Add the sour cream, parsley, onion, and horseradish and stir to blend. Cover and refrigerate until ready to use.

Brush the tenderloin with butter and season to taste with salt and pepper. Set aside.

Prepare a hot fire with a kiss of smoke (page 15) in your grill and add your desired type of wood.

When you see the first wisp of smoke from the wood, place the tenderloin on the grill. Close the lid and grill for 20 to 22 minutes, turning a quarter turn every 5 minutes and brushing with butter halfway through, or until a meat thermometer inserted in the thickest part of the tenderloin registers 130°F (50°C) for medium-rare, or until your desired doneness. Let rest for 5 minutes before slicing. Serve the sliced tenderloin with a dollop of the Bacon Mushroom Sauce on top or on the side.

PROVENÇAL BEEF DAUBE

A FRENCH *DAUBE* IS SIMILAR TO BRAISED *BOEUF BOURGUIGNON*, EXCEPT THE PIECES of beef are cut into larger cubes than for the bourguignon. The rich, fragrant broth gets a boost from smoking the meat first to add another layer of flavor. This *daube* is best made 2 days ahead and it is worth it. The first day, smoke the chuck roast for 1½ hours and marinate overnight. The second day, braise the beef in a fragrant, smoky broth, then let cool and refrigerate. The third day, you simply reheat the dish and serve with mashed potatoes, crusty bread and butter, and a hearty glass of red wine. It is a perfect make-ahead dish for company. To test whether the roast is fork-tender, stick a fork in a section of meat and twist. If the meat twists, it's tender enough. If you like, adding a simple, lightly dressed green salad completes this meal. As Julia Child would say, "Bon appétit!"

SERVES 8 TO 10

Suggested wood: Cherry, chestnut, or oak

4 pounds (2 kg) boneless beef chuck roast, cut into 3-inch (7.5-cm) cubes

4 white onions, thinly sliced (2 pounds/1 kg)

5 whole cloves

5 whole allspice

5 bay leaves

5 sprigs fresh thyme

4 cups (1 L) dry red wine

¼ cup (50 ml) olive oil

Kosher or sea salt and freshly ground black pepper

1 (28-ounce/800-g) can fire-roasted whole tomatoes with juice

1 (15-ounce/425-g) jar chopped roasted red bell peppers, drained

4 garlic cloves, minced

2 tablespoons drained capers

2 loaves of crusty bread, sliced

Prepare an indirect fire with a kiss of smoke (page 15) in your grill and add your desired type of wood. (Replenish the wood chips or chunks as necessary.)

Arrange the cubed beef in foil pan and place on the indirect side of the grill. Close the lid and smoke for 1½ hours.

Transfer the beef to a large stainless steel bowl. Cover with the onions and add cloves, allspice, bay leaves, and thyme. Pour the red wine over the meat mixture. Cover and refrigerate for 20 to 24 hours. Strain the beef mixture, reserving the marinade. Place the onions in a strainer and pat dry with paper towels. Using paper towels again, pat the cubed beef dry and set on a baking sheet on top of additional paper towels.

In a Dutch oven, heat oil over high heat and sauté the onions for 10 minutes, or until translucent. Remove with a slotted spoon to a plate and set aside.

Add oil to the pan if necessary and, working in three to four batches, brown the beef over medium heat, adding oil as necessary between batches. Season with salt and pepper, remove with a slotted spoon to a plate, and set aside.

Pour the marinade into the pan and bring to a boil. Reduce the heat to medium-low and add tomatoes with juice, roasted peppers, garlic, and capers. Return the onions, beef, and any accumulated juices to the pan. Cover and simmer for at least 2 hours, or until beef is fork-tender. Remove lid and let cool for at least 1 hour. Cover and refrigerate overnight.

To serve, reheat the *daube* and ladle three or four chunks of the beef with plenty of sauce and vegetables into each bowl. Serve the crusty bread in a basket. It's a must to sop up the delicious smoky gravy.

BEEF TENDERLOIN SAVOIR FAIRE

You can get extra savings on beef tenderloin if you trim it yourself. If you've ever trimmed out a pork tenderloin, the process is the same. The whole tenderloin will have a thick end and will taper down to a thin end. Trim off any fat and silverskin. If something looks like it isn't meat, trim it off. Tuck the tapered end under and tie the tenderloin at intervals with kitchen string so it is the same width and thickness all the way through. That way, it will grill evenly.

If you don't need a whole tenderloin for a dish, you can cut the size tenderloin you want to grill, and then slice the rest into 1-inch-thick (2.5 cm) filet mignons. Cut the tapered end into chunks for brochettes.

BISTRO STEAK WITH M. F. K. FISHER

Iconic food writer Mary Frances Kennedy Fisher lived in France, then wrote about her adventures for publications such as *House Beautiful*. In an article for that magazine in September 1944, she recounted the steak she had at a Parisian bistro owned by Madame Duflos. The steak, marinated in red wine vinegar and oil, would be patted dry, then "slapped onto a grill as hot as hell-fire and as searing," Fisher writes. "No turning-fork would ever prick it, and when it would finally be carved into long thin slices at the table, its juices would gush from it the color of garnets."

But that wasn't all. "The piles of watercress on the platter would be tossed in the cooling juices, and then served with the steak."

PORC
PORK

Certain regions of France are more known for their pork dishes than others. Normandy in northern France celebrates pork in sausages, pâté, and pork tenderloin cooked with apples. Alsace-Lorraine loves pork and sauerkraut, or roast pork with plums and cabbage. In the Loire Valley, pork loin is cooked with prunes.

Even ham shows regional preferences. Bayonne ham from the Pyrenees is brined with red wine and herbs, rubbed with a little Espelette (a dried red pepper), smoked for two weeks, then left to dry like an American country ham or prosciutto. Ham from the Ardennes is more heavily smoked. Ham from Paris is sweeter and more moist, like the traditional American Easter ham.

The recipes in this chapter show the regional flavors you'd find in bistro pork dishes but with the added flavor of the grill. Basque-Style Pork Paillards with Red Peppers (page 174) pair sweet pork with tangy peppers. Pork Chops Rapide get a Port Cherry Sauce (page 175). The light and elegant Pork Tenderloin Roulade with Frilly Greens and Fresh Herbs (page 179) is very different from the rich and meaty Grill-Roasted Pork Loin, Périgord-Style (page 181) that tastes of garlic and truffles.

Pork dishes with a French bistro twist are very much at home on the American grill.

BASQUE-STYLE PORK PAILLARDS WITH RED PEPPERS

THE BASQUE REGION IN THE SOUTHWESTERN PART OF FRANCE BORDERING SPAIN produces robust foods. Farm-fresh meats and day-boat fish are grilled over hot coals, and there is an abundance of tomatoes and sweet or hot red peppers in many dishes. Serve a triple recipe of Garden Tomato Salad (page 70) or Provençal Grill-Roasted Tomatoes (page 108) along with the pork. *Paillard* is French term meaning a very thin boneless, skinless piece of meat. On French bistro menus, you usually see chicken paillards, but at home you can easily make pork paillards from the loin. Cut ½ inch (1 cm) thick, pork paillards grill in just 5 minutes over a hot fire.

SERVES 6

2 pounds (1 kg) boneless pork loin, cut into ½-inch-thick (1 cm) steaks

Olive oil for brushing

Kosher or sea salt

Smoked paprika

4 red bell peppers, cored, seeded, and cut into eighths lengthwise (about 1½ pounds/750 g)

2 lemons, halved

2 tablespoons chopped fresh flat-leaf parsley

Prepare a hot fire in your grill.

Lightly brush the pork paillards with olive oil and season to taste with salt and smoked paprika. Set aside.

Lightly brush the pepper strips with olive oil and season to taste with salt.

Grill the pepper strips in an oiled grill wok or basket over the direct fire for about 10 to 12 minutes, tossing with long-handled wooden spoons in the grill wok or flipping the grill basket over from time to time.

Grill the pork paillards for 2½ minutes per side, turning once, until just a hint of pink remains inside.

Grill the lemon halves, cut-side down for about 2 or 3 minutes.

To serve, layer the pork paillards down the center of a platter and arrange the grilled pepper strips and lemon halves on either side. Squeeze some lemon juice over all and sprinkle the pork with the chopped parsley.

PORK CHOPS RAPIDE
WITH PORT CHERRY SAUCE

WHEN YOU ARE IN A HURRY, YOU DO NOT HAVE TO FORSAKE THE IDEA OF A delicious meal. Start at the butcher shop and buy four small butterflied pork chops, and then get a baguette at the bakery. Three different cheeses with Champagne grapes can do double duty as either an appetizer or as the cheese course after dinner. The Port Cherry Sauce ingredients can be staples in your pantry to whip up this sauce in less than 15 minutes—while the pork chops go on and off the grill. Serve the pork chops with a green salad and the rest of the evening is ooh-la-la!

SERVES 4

4 butterflied pork chops (6 ounces/175 g each), about ½ inch (1 cm) thick

Olive oil for brushing

Kosher or sea salt and freshly ground black pepper

Port Cherry Sauce

1 cup (175 g) dried, tart cherries

½ cup (125 ml) port wine

¼ cup (60 g) sugar

2 tablespoons freshly squeezed lemon juice

Prepare a medium-hot fire in your grill.

Lightly oil the pork chops and season with salt and pepper and set aside.

For the Port Cherry Sauce, bring ½ cup (125 ml) of water to a boil. Add the dried cherries and cook for 5 minutes over low heat until the cherries are plump. Add the port wine, sugar, and lemon juice to the pan and continue to simmer for 10 minutes or until the sauce slightly thickens. Remove from heat and set aside.

Grill the pork chops over the fire for about 2 minutes per side, turning only once. The chops should still be slightly pink in the center. Serve with the Port Cherry Sauce.

CHAR-GRILLED, THICK-CUT PORK CHOPS WITH CORN JAPONAISE

IN THE 1880s, ARTISTS CLAUDE MONET, EDWARD DEGAS, AND VINCENT VAN GOGH AS well as sculptor Auguste Rodin discovered and then collected Japanese prints. There was something about the Japanese aesthetic that appealed to them and influenced their work. Here, the Japanese flavor of miso—fermented soy that has a flavor like dried mushrooms or Worcestershire sauce—gives this bistro barbecue dish an exotic twist. Decadent, thick-cut pork chops are a main stay on restaurant and bistro menus. Sear these thick, bone-in chops over a medium-hot fire, and then finish them on the indirect side. Although corn is infrequently seen on Parisian bistro menus, we think that with a slather of White Miso Butter (page 47) it hits just the right flavor note. Keep the husks on the corn as you grill them. The heat from the grill makes the silks come right off when you peel back the husks, saving you the usual prep time of picking out those pesky strands of silk.

SERVES 4

4 (10-ounce/300-g) bone-in pork chops,
  about 1 inch (2.5 cm) thick

4 teaspoons olive oil

4 teaspoons Three-Peppercorn Rub (page 23)

4 ears fresh corn-on-the-cob in the husk,
  ½ pound (250 g) each

1 recipe White Miso Butter (page 47), prepared

Prepare a medium-hot indirect fire in your grill.

Brush the pork chops with olive oil and sprinkle with Three-Peppercorn Rub.

Grill for 4 minutes per side, rotating a quarter turn after 2 minutes on each side for crosshatch grill marks. Move the chops to the indirect side of the grill and close the lid. Grill for another 10 minutes or until a meat thermometer inserted in the thickest part of a chop registers 145°F (65°C) for medium-rare, or until desired doneness.

Grill the corn directly over the fire while you are grilling the pork chops. Turn the ears until the husks are browned, about 10 to 12 minutes. When ready to serve, pull the husks back to make a handle and serve with White Miso Butter for slathering on the corn, along with the peppery pork chops.

PORK TENDERLOIN ROULADE
WITH FRILLY GREENS AND FRESH HERBS

FORMAL. COMPOSED. AESTHETICALLY PLEASING. THAT'S THE FRENCH WAY. AND here is a grill version. A roulade—a boneless pork or turkey breast butterflied, pounded thin, stuffed, rolled, and grilled—looks beautiful when it is sliced into rounds so you can see the colors of the stuffing in spirals. You can have your butcher butterfly a pork tenderloin, but it's easy enough to do yourself. Simply cut each pork tenderloin halfway through, lengthwise, so you can open the tenderloin like a book. Using a meat mallet or a sturdy saucer, pound the butterflied tenderloin until it is an even thickness all the way through, about ½ inch (1 cm) thick. Served with a salad of Frilly Greens and Fresh Herbs, this is bistro barbecue meets *cuisine minceur* or healthy cooking.

SERVES 6

Suggested wood: Apple, almond, or oak

2 boneless pork tenderloins butterflied and pounded thin, 2 pounds (1 kg)

Kosher or sea salt and freshly ground black pepper

4 garlic cloves, slivered

3 tablespoons chopped fresh herb leaves like oregano, marjoram, chervil, and/or snipped chives

Olive oil for brushing

Kosher or sea salt and freshly ground black pepper

Frilly Greens and Fresh Herbs

2 cups (500 ml) fresh parsley leaves, torn from a large bunch of flat-leaf parsley

½ cup (125 ml) assorted fresh herb leaves like oregano, marjoram, chervil, and/or snipped chives

1 head green or red leaf lettuce, leaves freshly torn

1 small head of frisée, leaves freshly torn

1 tablespoon freshly squeezed lemon juice

1 tablespoon extra-virgin olive oil

Kosher or sea salt and freshly ground black pepper

Prepare an indirect fire with a kiss of smoke (page 15) in your grill and add your desired type of wood. (Replenish the wood chips as necessary.)

Lay each butterflied tenderloin, cut-side up, on a work surface and season with salt and pepper. Arrange the garlic evenly over the meat and sprinkle with fresh herbs. Starting with a long side, roll up jellyroll-style. Tie the roll together at intervals with kitchen string. Brush the exterior with olive oil and season with salt and pepper.

On the hot or direct side, grill the roulades for 2 minutes per side, turning a quarter turn at a time, or until the roulades have good grill marks.

Transfer the roulades to a disposable aluminum pan. When you see the first wisp of smoke, place the pan on the indirect side of the grill. Close the lid and smoke for about 1 to 1½ hours, or until a meat thermometer inserted in the thickest part of the meat registers 145°F (65°C) for medium-rare, or until your desired doneness. Transfer to a cutting board, tent with foil, and let rest for 10 minutes. (While the meat rests, it will continue to cook for another few degrees, so keep that in mind.)

To make the Frilly Greens and Fresh Herbs, place the herbs and lettuce in a large bowl. Drizzle with the lemon juice and olive oil. Season with salt and pepper and toss to lightly coat the greens.

To serve, slice the pork roulades into 1-inch-thick (2.5 cm) slices and serve with the herbs and greens on the side.

The tenderloins may also be refrigerated for up to 2 days and served cold.

VARIATION:

Instead of slow-smoked butterflied pork tenderloin roulades, simply season the whole pork tenderloins with salt and pepper and place in a large sealable plastic bag. Add the garlic and chopped herbs and drizzle with enough olive oil to lightly coat the pork. Refrigerate for 1 hour or up to 6 hours. Let the pork come to room temperature before grilling. Remove from marinade and grill over a medium-hot fire for 5 minutes per side, turning a quarter turn at a time or until a meat thermometer inserted into the thickest part of the tenderloin registers 145°F (65°C).

GRILL-ROASTED PORK LOIN, PÉRIGORD-STYLE

WHEN WE CAME ACROSS A RECIPE CALLED *ENCHAUD PÉRIGOURDIN* (POT ROAST Périgord-style) in Anne Willan's *French Regional Cooking*, we were struck by how delicious it would be on the grill. A pork loin, perfumed with slivers of garlic the night before, is grill-roasted to a juicy, caramelized turn. If you have a rotisserie attachment on your grill, see the variation on the next page on how to set that up. But you can simply place the pork loin on the indirect side of your grill and let it grill-roast until done. Périgord, in southwestern France, is a region known for duck confit, foie gras, and truffles. Indeed, writes Willan, the holiday version of this dish calls for the pork to be butterflied, pounded thin, spread with a truffled meat stuffing, then cooked. We simply slather this with White Truffle Aioli (page 31) as it grills.

SERVES 6

1 (3-pound/5-kg) boneless pork loin roast

Kosher or sea salt and
    freshly ground black pepper

3 large garlic cloves, cut into slivers

1 recipe White Truffle Aioli (page 31), prepared

1 teaspoon dried thyme

Fresh thyme sprigs, for garnish

The day before you want to grill, sprinkle the pork loin with salt and pepper. Using a paring knife, make small incisions in the surface of the meat and insert a sliver of garlic. Wrap the pork loin in plastic wrap and refrigerate to allow the garlic flavor to permeate the meat.

Prepare an indirect fire in your grill.

Unwrap the pork loin and place it in an aluminum pan. In a small bowl, mix the White Truffle Aioli with the dried thyme. Slather the surface of the meat with about a third of the White Truffle Aioli mixture. Place the pan on the indirect or no-heat side of the grill. Close the lid and grill-roast for 45 minutes. Open the lid and slather the pork loin with another third of the White Truffle Aioli mixture. Close the lid and grill-roast for another 45 minutes or until a meat thermometer inserted in the thickest part of the meat registers 145°F (65°C) for medium-rare, or until your desired doneness. Transfer to a cutting board, tent with foil, and let rest for 10 minutes.

Carve into slices and arrange them shingled, or overlapping, on a platter garnished with fresh thyme sprigs. Serve any remaining aioli alongside the pork.

VARIATION:

For Rotisserie Pork Loin, Périgord-Style, set up your grill for rotisserie grilling (page 18). Instead of placing the pork loin in a disposable aluminum pan, insert the rotisserie rod or spit through the center of the pork loin and attach the spit to the rotisserie. Slather the surface of the meat with about a third of the White Truffle Aioli mixture. Place a drip pan under the pork loin and fill it with water to reach a depth of 2 inches (5 cm). Prepare a medium-hot fire in your grill. Start the rotisserie and close the lid and grill-roast for 45 minutes. Open the lid and slather the pork loin with another third of the White Truffle Aioli mixture. Close the lid and grill-roast for another 45 minutes or until a meat thermometer inserted in the thickest part of the meat registers 145°F (65°C) for medium-rare, or until your desired doneness. Transfer to a cutting board, tent with foil, and let rest for 10 minutes.

Carve into slices and arrange them shingled, or overlapping, on a platter garnished with fresh thyme sprigs. Serve any remaining aioli alongside the pork.

SWEET AND STICKY RIBS

OUR COOKBOOK CLUB LOVED *LUNCH IN PARIS* BY ELIZABETH BARD. IT IS A LOVE story with the most delicious collection of recipes. We've adapted her oven-roasted rib recipe for the grill and added some traditional BBQ seasonings like celery salt and paprika. Serve the ribs with Grilled Red and Savoy Cabbage with Roquefort and Celery Seed Dressing (page 78) or a bistro salad of your choice. Use needle-nose pliers to grab the membrane on the underside of each rack of ribs and pull it off in one motion. This is easiest to do when the ribs are cold. Once they warm up, the membrane breaks apart, making it an exasperating task. One last tip—use two large aluminum foil pans placed one on top of the other for sturdier transport and holding of the ribs.

SERVES 6

1/2 cup (125 ml) dark honey

1/4 cup (50 ml) olive oil

1/4 cup (50 ml) red wine vinegar

2 garlic cloves, lightly crushed with
    the back of a knife

1 1/2 teaspoons celery salt

1 teaspoon paprika

4 pounds (2 kg) baby back ribs,
    trimmed and membrane removed

2 sprigs fresh rosemary

In a bowl, combine honey, oil, vinegar, garlic, celery salt, and paprika.

Cut the ribs into individual pieces and place in a large sealable plastic bag and pour in the marinade. Add the rosemary sprigs and seal the bag. Refrigerate for 1 1/2 hours, turning occasionally.

Prepare an indirect medium fire in your grill.

Pour the marinade from the ribs into a small saucepan and bring to a boil. Remove from the heat.

Arrange the ribs in a single layer in a large aluminum pan. Pour the hot marinade over the ribs.

Place the pan of ribs on the indirect side of the grill and grill-roast for about 2 to 2 1/2 hours, turning the ribs once or twice and turning the pan 180 degrees halfway through the roasting time. If the sticky sauce starts to get too brown your fire may be too hot. Turn down the fire and add a few spoonfuls of water to the sauce and stir to blend. The ribs are done when the meat at the ends of the ribs starts to pull away from the bone. Serve at once. Or refrigerate the ribs and serve cold the next day with buttered bread, pickles, and an ice-cold glass of Bière de Garde.

CHAPTER 13

POISSONS & CRUSTACÉ
FISH & SHELLFISH

Grilling fresh fish is the essence of fast French food, but grilling it requires a little savoir faire.

First, select the freshest fish. Look for whole fish with clear, not cloudy, eyes, or fresh fillets that have a fresh, briny aroma and a firm, not mushy, texture.

The rule of thumb for grilling fish *fillets* or steaks is 10 minutes per inch (2.5 cm) of thickness over a hot fire. That means that a fish fillet—usually about ¾ inch (2 cm) in the thickest part—will need to grill for about 3 to 4 minutes on each side. Some fish, like tuna in Bistro Tuna (page 189), taste best at rare or medium-rare, so the time on the grill is less. A very meaty fish like monkfish in Grilled Monkfish with Rouille (page 198) might take a little longer to get done.

It is better to oil the fish so it doesn't stick to the grill grates rather than oil the grill grates. Oiling the grill, then starting the fire, causes the oil to burn. When the oil burns off, the fish can stick to the grill grates.

Wire grilling baskets are great for grilling whole fish like Wood-Grilled Local Trout (page 192). You can grill fish fillets directly on the grill grates as in Grilled Halibut with Roasted Red Pepper Aioli (page 199), or grill tender fish fillets on a perforated grill rack.

On most fish fillets, there is a skin side (a darker side where the skin is or used to be) and a flesh side, which is lighter in color. Start grilling the fish flesh-side down, and then turn them over to the skin side. This helps the fish fillet hold together better during grilling.

Planking allows you the most effortless way to grill fish—it will have an aromatic flavor but no grill marks. Planked Cod with Dijon Mustard–Mayonnaise Slather (page 193) is so simple, you'll want to try this method for lots of other fish.

LOBSTER TAIL WITH PERNOD BUTTER

THE LIQUEUR PERNOD DATES BACK TO 1805 WHEN IT WAS FIRST DISTILLED WITH star anise and several herbs. To serve it as a drinking beverage, do as the French do and add cold water to it (similar to a pastis) or mix it with club soda. The slightly anise and tarragon-like flavor of Pernod Butter is delicious basted on the lobster tail.

SERVES 4

Pernod Butter

½ cup (113 g) unsalted butter, at room temperature

2 tablespoons Pernod liqueur

2 tablespoons dried tarragon

4 (8-ounce/230-g) rock lobster tails

4 tablespoons unsalted butter, at room temperature

Prepare a medium-hot fire in your grill.

For the Pernod Butter, combine the butter, Pernod, and tarragon in a bowl until smooth. Set aside.

Cut the top membrane from the lobster tails and discard. Loosen the lobster meat from the shell and brush with room-temperature butter.

Place the lobster tails on the grill grates, cut-side down, and grill for 2 to 3 minutes or until they have grill marks. Turn the tails and grill until done, 7 to 9 minutes. The lobster meat will be opaque and the shell will be charred. Serve with the extra Pernod Butter.

VARIATIONS:

Serve the hot grilled lobster with other butters like Lemon-Herb Butter (page 104) or Tarragon Butter (page 106). Or make extra lobster to chill and serve the next day as a cold lobster salad with Hollandaise Sauce (page 35) or White Truffle Aioli (page 31) on the side.

GRILLED SCALLOPS WITH FENNEL, RED PEPPER, AND LEMON-TARRAGON VINAIGRETTE

SEA SCALLOPS ARE THOSE LUSCIOUS LARGE SCALLOPS THAT YOU FIND ON JUST about every fine dining restaurant menu. With this dish's eye-popping presentation and flavor, you won't believe how easy it is to make. We got the original idea from California chef John Ash and took it from there. Each serving is for three large sea scallops, so buy more if you desire a larger serving.

SERVES 4

1 large fennel bulb (8 ounces/250 g), trimmed, quartered, and sliced 1/4 inch (0.5 cm) thick

2 large red bell peppers (6 ounces/175 g each), cored, seeded, and cut into strips

About 2 tablespoons olive oil, plus more for brushing

Kosher or sea salt and freshly ground black pepper

12 large sea scallops, 1 1/2 to 2 inches (4 to 5 cm) in diameter

3/4 cup (175 ml) Lemon-Tarragon Vinaigrette (page 26), prepared

Tarragon sprigs, for garnish

Prepare a hot fire in your grill.

Oil a grill wok or perforated grill rack. Toss the fennel and red pepper strips with the olive oil in a bowl and season with salt and pepper. Place the vegetables in the wok or on the grill rack. Grill for about 10 minutes, turning the vegetables every few minutes until they are scorched and tender. Transfer the vegetables to a platter. Brush the scallops on both sides with olive oil and season with salt and pepper. Grill the scallops directly on the grill grates for about 3 minutes per side or until they are opaque but still a little translucent in the center.

To serve, divide the fennel slices and pepper strips among four plates, place three scallops on each plate, and drizzle with Lemon-Tarragon Vinaigrette. Garnish with fresh tarragon sprigs and serve immediately.

BISTRO TUNA

TWO PANTRY RECIPES ARE INCLUDED IN THIS SIMPLE QUICK-TO-GRILL TUNA. THE *truc* is to make the peppercorn rub first, then you have the peppercorns ready to use in the beurre blanc. Tuna is usually served rare to medium-rare, so if you like yours more done, you'll need to grill it longer. Swordfish would be a great substitute for the tuna. Be careful not to overcook swordfish or it becomes tough and dry. Make the Three-Peppercorn Beurre Blanc while the grill is heating up and keep it warm over a pan of hot water until you finish grilling the tuna.

SERVES 4

4 (6-ounce/175-g) tuna steaks,
   1 inch (2.5 cm) thick

2 tablespoons olive oil

1 recipe Three-Peppercorn Rub
   (page 23), prepared

2 lemons, halved

1 (12-ounce/175-g) package mixed
   fresh baby greens

1 recipe Three-Peppercorn Beurre Blanc
   (page 39), prepared and kept warm

Prepare a hot fire in your grill.

Lightly brush the tuna steaks with olive oil. Spread about 2 tablespoons of rub on a plate and lightly press both sides of the tuna steaks into the peppercorns.

Grill the tuna for about 3 minutes per side for rare. (Note the short cooking time; tuna will toughen if overcooked.) Place the lemons on grill, cut-side down, when you turn the tuna, and grill them for 3 minutes until warm and slightly charred.

Serve the tuna over the greens, squeezing the lemons over the tuna, and then spoon the Three-Peppercorn Beurre Blanc over the tuna.

SKATE WING
WITH BROWNED BUTTER AND CAPERS

SKATE IS DELICIOUS, AND THIS IS THE CLASSIC WAY TO SERVE IT. SKATE HAS A TENdency to get sticky, so use a perforated grill rack and let it heat up as the grill heats up. Bistros tend to serve boiled potatoes with this dish—something to soak up all that delicious *beurre noisette*—but why not grill fingerlings along with the skate and have the best of both worlds?

SERVES 4

⅔ cup (150 g) unsalted butter

4 (8-ounce/250-g) skate wings,
   cleaned and skinned

2 lemons, halved

¼ cup (50 ml) olive oil

1 pound fingerling potatoes,
   rinsed and patted dry

Kosher or sea salt and
   freshly ground black pepper

2 tablespoons capers

2 tablespoons chopped fresh
   flat-leaf parsley leaves

Prepare a hot fire in your grill.

While the grill is heating up, make the browned butter. In a small saucepan, heat the butter over medium heat until it foams and turns a rich nutty brown. Remove from the heat.

Place the skate wings and the halved lemons on a large platter and liberally coat the fish with olive oil. Toss the fingerling potatoes with about 2 tablespoons of the olive oil in a large bowl and season with salt and pepper.

Grill the fingerlings in a perforated grill basket or an aluminum pan with holes in it. Place over the hot fire and close the grill lid. After about 3 or 4 minutes, open the grill and toss the potatoes. Close the lid again and repeat the tossing in about another 3 or 4 minutes. Cook until the potatoes are tender when pierced with a fork. Transfer to a serving platter and arrange around the perimeter of the platter. Grill the skate wings until they just begin to flake when tested with a fork, 4 to 5 minutes on each side. At the same time, grill the lemon halves, cut-side down, for about 3 minutes until warmed through and lightly browned.

Transfer the skate to the middle of the serving platter, season with salt and pepper, and sprinkle on the capers and parsley. Place the grilled lemon halves on the platter, too.

Drizzle the browned butter over the skate, squeeze one of the lemon halves over the fish, and serve immediately.

HERB-GRILLING FISH

In seaside towns in the south of France, grilling fish over dried stalks of wild fennel perfumes the air—and the fish—with a sweet herby flavor. If you want to be very authentic, you can grow wild fennel in your garden from seed. Seeds of Italy at www.growitalian.com offers the Mediterranean wild fennel known as *finocchio selvatico*, which produces flavorful leaves and seeds but does not bulb as the vegetable fennel does. You can also use dried stalks of lavender, thyme, rosemary, lemon balm, lemon verbena, or sage.

To herb grill, prepare a hot fire in your grill.

For a charcoal grill, put the five to six dried herb stalks directly on ashed-over coals and replace the grill grate.

For a gas grill, crumble up the dried herb stalks and place them in a metal smoker box or make an aluminum foil packet (with holes punched in it so the smoke can escape). Place the smoker box or foil packet near a burner.

When you see the first wisp of smoke, put the fish fillet on the grill grates, close the lid, and grill 3 to 4 minutes without turning. Lift the lid, quickly turn the fish, and grill for 3 to 4 minutes more with the lid closed or until the fish is done to your liking.

Herb-grilled fish is delicious served with Hollandaise Sauce (page 35), Béarnaise Sauce (page 36), Mustard-Cornichon Beurre Blanc (page 38), Food Processor Aioli (page 29), or Rouille (page 198).

WOOD-GRILLED LOCAL TROUT

THERE ARE FEW RECIPES QUITE AS SIMPLE AND DELICIOUS AS THIS ONE. WHOLE trout are stuffed with butter, lemon, and herbs, and then grilled over aromatic wood. Use a fish basket, or a wide fish spatula, or two grill spatulas to turn the fish on the grill grates. You can fillet the cooked fish in the kitchen before serving or serve intact and let diners remove the skin and bones.

SERVES 4

Suggested wood: Apple, maple, or oak

4 whole trout, cleaned
(about 12 ounces/375 g each)

½ cup (113 g) unsalted butter, melted

2 lemons, thinly sliced

1 cup (30 g) mixed fresh herbs,
such as basil, parsley, dill, and chives

Kosher or sea salt and
freshly ground black pepper

Prepare a medium-hot fire with a kiss of smoke (page 15) in your grill and add your desired type of wood.

Open each trout like a book and brush with butter. Arrange the lemon slices and herbs on one side and season with salt and pepper. Close the trout and brush the exterior with butter. Place the fish on a baking sheet to take out to the grill.

When you see the first wisp of smoke from the wood, transfer the fish from the baking sheet to the grill grates. Close the lid and grill for 25 to 30 minutes, turning the fish every 8 minutes, until the fish is opaque and flakes easily with a fork.

VARIATION:

Omit the butter and wrap each fish in bacon or pancetta, securing the meat with toothpicks.

PLANKED COD
WITH DIJON MUSTARD–MAYONNAISE SLATHER

PLANKING FISH OR SHELLFISH IS ONE OF THE EASIEST, MOST FOOLPROOF WAYS TO grill seafood. The fish won't fall through the grill grates, and you don't have to turn it. This technique is perfect for delicate fillets like turbot, flounder, tilapia, or sole. You can plank almost any fish or shellfish, but for the best outcome, choose varieties that are not more than 1 inch (2.5 cm) thick, so that you get more flavor from the wood underneath. For maximum flavor, the flesh should touch the wood plank, so purchase skinless fish or skin it yourself. With planking, as with grilling, the thickness of the fish (measured at the thickest part) determines the timing. A ¾-inch thick (2 cm) fillet will take 25 to 30 minutes using this indirect method. The slather ensures that you'll have a flavorful moist fish.

SERVES 6

One 15 x 6½ x 8 inch (37 x 16 x 20 cm) cedar or alder grilling plank, soaked in water for at least 1 hour

One ¾-inch-thick (2 cm) skinless cod fillet, 1½ to 2 pounds (750 g to 1 kg)

1 cup (250 ml) Dijon Mustard–Mayonnaise Slather (page 28), prepared

Zest and juice of ½ lemon

Prepare an indirect hot fire in your grill.

Compare the length of the plank with the length of the cod fillet and trim the cod to fit the plank, if necessary. Place the cod on the prepared plank and spread the mustard slather over the top and sides, sealing the edges to the plank.

Place the plank on the indirect side of the grill. Close the grill lid and cook for 15 minutes. Turn the plank 180 degrees and close the lid again. Cook for another 15 minutes until the fish begins to flake when tested with a fork in the thickest part, about 30 minutes total. Serve the cod right from the plank sprinkled with the lemon zest and drizzled with the lemon juice.

VERMOUTH SMOKED SALMON
WITH JUNIPER BERRIES

VERMOUTH IS A FORTIFIED WINE THAT IS ALSO GENTLY AROMATIZED AND FLAVORED with herbs and spices. Noilly Pratt was the first pale, dry vermouth made in France, and it's the classic vermouth to use for a martini. Since you'll have a bottle for this recipe, serve it as an aperitif on the rocks with a twist of lemon, or whip up a batch of martinis to serve while you tend the fish. The salmon comes out tender, moist, and smoky. Serve it simply with grilled asparagus and classic Hollandaise Sauce (page 35).

SERVES 4

Suggested wood: Alder or oak

¼ cup (50 ml) gin or vodka

¼ cup (50 ml) dry white vermouth

¼ cup (50 ml) freshly squeezed lemon juice

3 tablespoons unsalted butter, melted

1 tablespoon prepared horseradish

½ teaspoon hot sauce

1 garlic clove, minced

2 tablespoons juniper berries,
 plus more for garnish

1 salmon fillet (1½ to 2 pounds/.75 to 1 kg),
 skin on or off

1 lemon, sliced, plus more for garnish

6 sprigs fresh dill, plus more for garnish

Prepare a medium-low indirect fire with a kiss of smoke (page 15) in your grill and add your desired type of wood. (Replenish the wood chips as necessary.)

In a small saucepan, combine the gin, vermouth, lemon juice, butter, horseradish, hot sauce, garlic, and juniper berries and bring to a boil. Set aside.

Place the salmon in an aluminum pan large enough to hold the fish. Place the lemon slices and sprigs of dill on top of the salmon. Pour the vermouth baste over the salmon and cover with foil.

Place the salmon on the indirect side of your grill, close the lid, and smoke for 1 hour. Remove the foil and smoke until the salmon is opaque and begins to flake when tested with a fork, about 15 to 30 minutes more.

Serve the salmon on a platter garnished with more lemon slices, fresh dill, and juniper berries. It is tasty warm or cold and would make wonderful smoky salmon tartines with a dollop of Smoked Garlic Aioli (page 29).

GRILLED SALMON
WITH AVOCADO CRÈME FRAÎCHE

WHEN FRESH SALMON IS IN SEASON, GRILL A WHOLE FILLET TO SERVE WITH this lime-and-cilantro-scented sauce. It's always better to under-grill fish than to overcook it. You can always put the fish back on the grill or pop it in the oven to finish, but a dry and overcooked fish can't be rescued. With a platter of fresh tomatoes or one of our bistro salads, this is healthy eating or *cuisine minceur*, the *BBQ Bistro* way.

SERVES 6 TO 8

1 salmon fillet (3 to 3½ pounds/1.5 to 1.75 kg)

Olive oil for brushing

Kosher or sea salt and
   freshly ground black pepper

Lime slices and cilantro sprigs, for garnish

1 recipe Avocado Crème Fraîche
   (page 33), prepared

Prepare a hot fire in your grill.

Brush the salmon with olive oil, then season with salt and pepper. Place on a baking sheet and take out to the grill.

Grill the salmon, flesh-side down, for 3 to 4 minutes. Using two grill or fish spatulas, loosen the salmon from the grill grates and carefully roll it over, so the skin side is down. Grill for another 3 to 4 minutes, until it just begins to flake when tested with a fork in the thickest part. Serve the salmon on a platter garnished with lime slices and cilantro sprigs. Pass the Avocado Crème Fraîche separately.

FRENCH 75

Cocktails anyone? We couldn't have an American grilling book with a French flair without this classic drink created at the New York Bar in Paris in 1915, which later became Harry's New York Bar. The kick you get from this drink was said to feel like being shelled with a French 75mm field gun. Half fill a cocktail shaker with a jigger of gin, 1 teaspoon simple syrup, juice of half a lemon, and cracked ice. Shake vigorously and pour the liquid into a champagne flute and top with chilled Champagne. Bombs away!

GRILLED MONKFISH WITH ROUILLE

THICK AND MEATY, MONKFISH HAS BEEN CALLED "POOR MAN'S LOBSTER" FOR GOOD reason: It has a similar texture without being as sweet. It is very easy to grill since it doesn't fall apart on the grill like other flaky fin fish, but you do need to make sure it is cooked all the way through or it can be rubbery if undercooked. Here it's paired with rouille, the classic Mediterranean garlic and saffron mayonnaise. The rouille can be stored in an airtight container in the refrigerator for up to 4 days. Be sure to serve some crusty French bread that's been heated up on the grill to dredge in the extra rouille. Why not grill a few other vegetables along with the fish and then enjoy those with the rouille as well?

SERVES 6 TO 8

Rouille

4 garlic cloves

4 large egg yolks, at room temperature

$1/4$ teaspoon saffron threads

$1/4$ teaspoon kosher or sea salt

$1/4$ teaspoon ground red pepper

1 cup (250 ml) extra-virgin olive oil

$2^{1}/2$ pounds (1.25 kg) skinless monkfish fillets

Olive oil for brushing

Kosher or sea salt and
  freshly ground black pepper

For the Rouille, combine the garlic, egg yolks, saffron, salt, and pepper in a food processor and process until smooth. With the motor running, through the feed tube, gradually add olive oil in a steady stream until the mixture thickens. Cover and refrigerate until ready to use.

Prepare a medium-hot indirect fire in your grill.

Brush the fish with olive oil and season with salt and pepper.

Grill the fish for 12 minutes per 1 inch (2.5 cm) of thickness, turning every 3 or 4 minutes, until the fish is lightly charred, cooked through, and tender. Slice the monkfish at an angle and serve each portion with a dollop of Rouille.

GRILLED HALIBUT
WITH ROASTED RED PEPPER AIOLI

A GRILLED HALIBUT FILLET MAKES A GREAT PRESENTATION ON A PLATTER. Remember to grill for 10 minutes per 1 inch (2.5 cm) of thickness, turning only once. The Roasted Red Pepper Aioli is quick to make using store-bought mayonnaise and keeps in the refrigerator for about 1 week. You can use store-bought roasted peppers in a jar, roast your own, or make use of your Grill Pantry (page 37). To roast peppers, preheat your grill to high. Grill whole peppers until blackened, blistered, and tender. Place peppers in a brown paper bag and close the top. Set aside for about 5 minutes until cool. Slice peppers open to remove the core and seeds. Rub excess char off the skins. Use immediately or store in an airtight container in the refrigerator for up to 2 days.

SERVES 6

Roasted Red Pepper Aioli

2 garlic cloves, chopped

1 (6-ounce/175-g) red bell pepper, grilled or roasted (about 1/2 cup/125 ml from a jar)

1 1/2 cups (375 ml) mayonnaise

1 to 2 tablespoons freshly squeezed lemon juice

2 pounds (1 kg) skinless halibut fillet

Olive oil for brushing

Kosher or sea salt and freshly ground black pepper

3 lemons, halved

Chopped fresh flat-leaf parsley, for garnish

For the Roasted Red Pepper Aioli, purée the garlic, pepper, and mayonnaise in a food processor until smooth. Transfer to a bowl and stir in lemon juice to taste. Cover and refrigerate until ready to use.

Prepare a hot fire in your grill.

Lightly brush the fish with olive oil and season with salt and pepper.

Place the fish, flesh-side down, on the grill. Grill for 10 minutes per inch (25-cm) of thickness, turning once, until the fish is opaque and flakes easily with a fork.

Grill the lemon halves at the same time, cut-side down, for about 5 minutes or until nicely browned.

Place the halibut fillet on a platter and surround with grilled lemon halves. Spoon the pinkish-tinged aioli down the center of the fillet, and then sprinkle with bright green parsley.

CHAPTER 14

LES DESSERTS & LES FRUITS FRAIS
DESSERT & FRUITS

Fresh fruit is a lovely and lighter way to end a meal, especially if the fruit caramelizes—just a little—on the grill.

Naturally soft fruits, such as apricots, peaches, plums, figs, and nectarines, are best grilled cut in half. Firmer fruits, such as apples and pears, can be cut in half, sliced, or cored, and cut into rings or wedges for grilling. Clusters of grilled grapes make a wonderful addition to a cheese platter or a light dessert with Brown Sugar Crème Fraîche (page 33).

The simplest way to prepare whole or cut fruit for grilling is cook it naked over the fire. If you like, you can brush it with mild olive oil (not extra-virgin), grapeseed oil, or other vegetable oil. Melted butter is also delicious; it won't have time to burn, because you grill fruit for only a few minutes per cut side.

As quickly as fruit grills, so does bread. Make sure to try some of the Dessert Tartines (page 211) for grilled baguette or brioche with sweet dessert toppings. Also, the Homemade Refrigerator Jam (page 208) is a quick jam that you can make in about 20 minutes. It will make you feel so smug serving this to your friends.

And then you have a new pantheon of French dessert accompaniments to serve with your grilled fruit. Sauce Normande (page 202), flavored with Calvados and cream, is wonderful with grilled apples. Fresh raspberries crushed with crème de cassis update a Grilled Pêche Melba (page 203). And Almond Chantilly, or almond-flavored sweetened whipped cream, is delightful with Grilled Apricot and Plum Skewers (page 204).

GRILLED APPLE RINGS
WITH SAUCE NORMANDE

FOR EATING OUT OF HAND, YOU WANT A CRISP, TART APPLE. BUT FOR GRILLING, YOU want a softer, sweeter apple, such as a Golden Delicious, that will soften but not crack or fall apart. These grilled apple slices go well for dessert or they pair as a side dish with grilled or smoked game birds, poultry, or pork. If you like, serve these grilled apple rings with a frozen treat with the flavors of autumn—cinnamon, pumpkin spice, or caramel ice cream. Drizzle extra Sauce Normande over all.

SERVES 4

Sauce Normande

½ cup (125 ml) apple cider

½ cup (125 ml) heavy whipping cream

1 tablespoon (or more) Calvados, applejack, or bourbon

4 Golden Delicious apples
   (about 1½ pounds/750 g)

For the Sauce Normande, pour the apple cider into a small saucepan and bring to a boil over high heat; boil until reduced by half, about 4 minutes. Remove from the heat and stir in the cream and Calvados. Set aside.

Prepare a medium-hot fire in your grill.

Using an apple corer, remove cores from the apples. Cut the apples into 1-inch-thick (2.5 cm) rings. Place the rings on a baking sheet and brush one side with some of the sauce. Place the apples, basted-side down, on the grill. Grill for 5 to 7 minutes, basting with the sauce and turning once, until the apples have good grill marks on both sides. Serve warm or at room temperature with additional sauce drizzled over all.

VARIATION:

Pears, nectarines, plums, and peaches are also good grilled with this sauce. Simply pit the fruit, cut it into quarters, brush with the sauce, and grill.

GRILLED PÊCHE MELBA
WITH CRUSHED RASPBERRIES AND CRÈME DE CASSIS

AUGUSTE ESCOFFIER CREATED PEACH MELBA IN HONOR OF AUSTRALIAN OPERA singer Nellie Melba, and it has become a classic. Celebrate any occasion with our grilled version when fresh, juicy peaches are at summer's peak of ripeness. On the grill they get a boost of warmth and caramelization. The crushed raspberries are simple to prepare without forsaking a soupçon of flavor.

SERVES 4 TO 8

2 cups (500 ml) raspberries

2 to 3 tablespoons crème de cassis
   or raspberry liqueur

Pinch of sea salt

4 large firm, ripe peaches or nectarines,
   unpeeled and halved
   (about 1½ pounds/750 g)

1 quart (1 L) French vanilla ice cream

Prepare the raspberries by placing them in a small bowl. Crush the raspberries and stir in the crème de cassis and salt. Set aside.

Prepare a medium-hot fire in your grill.

Place the peaches, cut-side down, on the grill. Grill for 4 to 6 minutes, on one side only, until the peaches are tender and blistered.

Arrange the peaches on a platter or portion into shallow glass bowls. Spoon the crushed raspberries over the peaches. Serve with a scoop of vanilla ice cream.

GRILLED APRICOT AND PLUM SKEWERS WITH ALMOND CHANTILLY

FRESH APRICOTS USUALLY PROMISE MORE THAN THEY CAN DELIVER, BUT NOT IN this recipe. For a fetching rustic look for this delicious dessert, choose sturdy lavender branches or campfire sticks and apricots and plums that are about the same size. If using lavender branches, there may be room for only one fruit per branch. Make sure to strip 2 or 3 inches (5 or 7.5 cm) of lavender leaves off the bottom of the branch. The branches or sticks should be fresh and green inside so they don't burn; if they are dry, soak them for 30 minutes before skewering the fruit.

SERVES 8

8 lavender branches or campfire sticks about 6 to 8 inches (15 to 20 cm) long

Almond Chantilly

1 cup (250 ml) heavy whipping cream

2 tablespoons granulated sugar

½ teaspoon almond extract

8 firm apricots, halved (about 2 pounds/1 kg)

8 firm purple plums, halved (about 2 pounds/1 kg)

¼ cup (56 g) butter, melted

1 cup (140 g) blackberries, for garnish

Prepare a medium-hot fire in your grill.

For the Almond Chantilly, beat the cream, sugar, and almond extract in a bowl with an electric mixer until stiff peaks form. Set aside. Keep cold.

Thread the apricots and plums on branches or sticks so that they look like whole fruit, two cut sides together, leaving space between the "whole" fruits. Brush with butter.

Grill the skewers for 6 to 8 minutes, turning often, until the fruit begins to soften and has a scorched exterior. Serve each skewer with a dollop of Almond Chantilly and a scattering of blackberries.

GRILLED POUND CAKE
WITH STRAWBERRY COMPOTE

A TRADITIONAL POUND CAKE IS CALLED *QUATRE-QUARTS* OR FOUR-FOURTHS IN French, meaning it has equal weights of butter, flour, sugar, and eggs in the recipe. Whether you make your own or buy a pound cake, this dessert is perfect in the spring or summer. Melt your favorite kind of jam, such as strawberry or blackberry, add the grated zest and juice of 1 lemon and some fresh crushed berries, and you have compote! This can do double duty as a dessert or a breakfast dish.

SERVES 8 TO 12

Strawberry Compote

1 pound (450 g) strawberries

¼ cup (50 ml) strawberry jam or preserves

1 lemon

1 pound cake (store-bought or homemade), cut into ½-inch-thick (1 cm) slices

¼ cup (125 g) melted butter

8 to 12 sprigs of fresh mint, for garnish

For the Strawberry Compote, hull the strawberries and slice in half. In a small saucepan, melt the jam and add the zest and juice of the lemon. Add half the strawberries and simmer for about 5 minutes, crushing the strawberries and stirring until it is somewhat thick. Remove from the heat and add the rest of the strawberries and stir to coat. Set aside.

Prepare a medium-hot fire in your grill.

Brush the pound cake lightly with butter on both sides. Grill for 2 to 3 minutes, turning once, until there are light golden brown grill marks on both sides. Serve the grilled pound cake with spoonfuls of the Strawberry Compote and top each dessert with a sprig of fresh mint.

VARIATION:

Substitute angel food cake for the pound cake, but it do not brush it with butter. The angel food cake will get nice grill marks in 1 to 2 minutes. Serve with Strawberry Compote, a scoop of vanilla or strawberry ice cream, and a sprig of mint. Pistachio ice cream would be sensational, too.

GRILLED FIGS AND PEARS
WITH BROWN SUGAR CRÈME FRAÎCHE

FRESH GREEN CALIMYRNA FIGS ARE ESPECIALLY NICE FOR THIS DISH. NECTARINES, peaches, and apples would all be interesting substitutes for the figs. Pit or core the fruit and cut into quarters. Honeyed crème fraîche (just add a small amount of honey to crème fraîche) or the Almond Chantilly (page 33) would be nice toppings, too.

SERVES 4

¼ cup (50 ml) wildflower honey

Grated zest of 1 orange

6 fresh Calimyrna or Mission figs, halved lengthwise (about 2 pounds/1 kg)

2 pears cored and halved lengthwise (about 14 ounces/435 g)

1 teaspoon chopped fresh rosemary

Brown Sugar Crème Fraîche (page 33), prepared

4 sprigs fresh rosemary, for garnish

Prepare a hot fire in your grill.

In a bowl, combine the honey and orange zest. Set aside.

Grill figs and pears cut-side down for about 3 or 4 minutes or until there are good grill marks. Turn fruit over and close the grill lid. Grill for 2 or 3 minutes more until warmed all the way through.

Place the grilled figs and pears on a platter. Drizzle with orange honey and sprinkle with chopped rosemary and dollops of Brown Sugar Crème Fraîche. Garnish with the rosemary sprigs.

HOMEMADE REFRIGERATOR JAM

Partly a sauce, partly a spoonable jam, this flavorful and colorful treat keeps for about a week in the refrigerator.

BUTTER-GRILLED BRIOCHE
WITH HOMEMADE REFRIGERATOR JAM

For the brioche, butter the slices of brioche and grill for a couple of minutes on each side for a golden brown toast.

For the homemade refrigerator jam, in a small saucepan combine the juice and zest of 1 lemon, 1½ cups (375 ml) sugar (or less if you like it less sweet), and 1 teaspoon instant tapioca and cook slow over medium-low heat. Add 3 cups (750 ml) of chopped fruit or berries like peaches, nectarines, apricots, pears, or berries and simmer for about 15 to 20 minutes until the mixture thickens. Add a squeeze or two of freshly squeezed lemon juice and stir. Spoon the warm jam over the grilled brioche and smile.

The jam will keep for 7 to 10 days in the refrigerator.

DESSERT TARTINES

Remember when you were little and a special treat was cinnamon toast? It was good for breakfast, a snack, or even for dessert. In Belgium, homemade buttered bread served with chocolate sprinkles is *the* childhood snack. And when our cookbook club read *Cooking for Mr. Latte*, we fell in love with Amanda Hesser's "Toasts with Chocolate and Fleur de Sel." So here are some wonderful blueprint recipes for grilled baguette or brioche with sweet dessert toppings. Many of the toppings that accompany the fruit in this chapter are delicious on tartines, too, like the peaches and raspberries from Grilled Pêche Melba with Crushed Raspberries and Crème de Cassis (page 203).

A baguette or loaf of brioche forms the base of the tartine. Slice the baguettes on the diagonal about ½ inch (1 cm) thick. Slice the brioche about ½ inch (1 cm) thick. Lightly brush the bread with olive oil or melted butter. Grill over a hot fire until you get good grill marks, about 2 or 3 minutes per side.

Then add any of the following toppings:

CHOCOLATE TARTINE: Place a piece of dark chocolate on top of the toasted bread and place on the indirect side of your grill with the lid closed for about 2 or 3 minutes until the chocolate melts. Sprinkle with a few grains of fleur de sel and serve.

STRAWBERRY TARTINE: Serve the toasted bread with a bowl of Strawberry Compote (page 207) for spooning on top.

HAZELNUT TARTINE: Serve the toasted bread with Nutella or other chocolate hazelnut spread and sprinkle with chopped, toasted hazelnuts and shaved dark chocolate.

GRILLED APPLE NORMANDE TARTINE: Place two Grilled Apple Rings (page 202) on each tartine and drizzle with more Sauce Normande.

GRILLED APPLE TARTINE WITH SALTED CARAMEL SAUCE: Place two Grilled Apple Rings (page 202) on each tartine and drizzle with warm caramel sauce and a sprinkle of fleur de sel.

GRILLED TARTINE WITH PEACHES, RED ONION, AND BASIL: Place two thin slices of red onion and two or three juicy peach slices on the toasted bread. Garnish with freshly chopped basil (or mint if you'd rather).

BROWN SUGAR CRÈME FRAÎCHE TARTINE: Dollop Brown Sugar Crème Fraîche (page 33) on each tartine and sprinkle with fresh raspberries or blueberries.

SPOON JAM TARTINE: Serve the toasted bread with your favorite homemade or high-quality jams or preserves with a dollop of Almond Chantilly (page 204).

LEMON CURD TARTINE: Serve the toasted bread with your favorite lemon curd, homemade or store-bought. Top with berries, sliced peaches, whipped cream, or all of these!

ACKNOWLEDGMENTS

A special *merci beaucoup* to agents Lisa Ekus and Sally Ekus, our editors, Kristen Wiewora and Sophia Muthuraj, Carolyn Sobczak, Martha Whitt, and everyone at Running Press who had a hand in the success of this wonderful cookbook. We want to thank Anne Willan, who opened Chateau du Fey in Burgundy to us, Kathie Alex who let us channel Julia Child at La Pitchoune in Provence, and bistro chefs all over France. Thanks to Mary Ann Duckers for getting the recipes in great shape and our taste-testing families for letting us know if we were on the right track.

INDEX